About the Book

Even the Indians of the desolate region of the Grand Canyon avoided the violent Green and Colorado Rivers. Charting them was an incredible feat that is sometimes referred to as the final chapter in the history of exploration in the American West. It did not take place until 1869, when a one-armed geology professor from the midwest, Major John Wesley Powell, led a small expedition through the treacherous 1000-mile boulder-strewn course where giant rapids threatened to capsize the small boats and hurl the men against the rocks. This biography of Powell records this 99-day life-and-death journey in vivid detail.

John Wesley Powell
CONQUEST OF THE CANYON
by Vada F. Carlson

drawings by Richard Cuffari

Harvey House, Inc.
Publishers
Irvington-on-Hudson, N.Y.

Library of Congress Catalog Card Number 73-79453
Manufactured in the United States of America
ISBN 0-8178-5131-3, Trade Edition. ISBN 0-8178-5132-1, Library Edition

Harvey House, Inc., Publishers
Irvington, New York 10533

Table of Contents

1

Big River Bad Medicine

THE LONG, SHRILL WHISTLE echoed against red sandstone cliffs that towered behind a tiny cluster of shacks. A freight train was passing through Green River City, Wyoming. The sound shattered the quiet of the spring morning and Major John Wesley Powell, busy supervising the loading of four new river boats, paused to listen until the rumbling faded into the distance. Then he went back to work, little hampered by the lack of a right forearm. A man of tremendous will and excellent health at thirty-five, he merely made his left arm do the work of two.

"You're not likely to hear another train whistle for some time," he called to the men loading the boats, "but you'll have this to remember on lonely nights in the canyons."

Walter Powell, the major's brother, laughed. "I should think we'll be too tired at night to get lonesome." He gave a slight nod toward the town. "Look who's coming."

The approaching riders were more in keeping with the desolation of the small settlement than was its new railway, whose steel rails had only recently been laid down along the trails of pioneer wagon trains. Just weeks before, civilization had broken through to the Pacific coast with the driving of the Golden Spike at Promontory Point, Utah. In 1869, however, Green River City was still as rough and forlorn as the two bedraggled Indians who turned down to the snow-fed Green River where Major Powell's boats were beached.

An old man with gray braids hanging over his shoulders led the way. He rode a sagging pinto pony without a saddle, his thin legs and mocca-

sined feet dangling. The younger man was dressed as a cowboy with an Indian beaded band around his high-crowned hat.

They reined up slowly and sat staring at the men, who were absorbed in the task of transferring piled-up supplies from the river bank to the boats. The old man spoke at length to his companion, who dismounted and strolled over to the soldierly leader.

" 'Morning," Powell greeted him. "What's on your mind?"

The young Indian looked down at the toes of his boots and mumbled, "My father say — where you go in boats?"

Powell might have told him that he was about to embark on one of the most dangerous journeys ever attempted. Instead he said calmly, "Tell him we are going through the Grand Canyon of the Colorado."

The young man raised his head and glanced from Powell's handsome bearded face to his empty sleeve. Then he turned to speak to his father who slid stiffly from his saddle blanket and hobbled down the bank to join them, talking all the while.

"What's he saying?" asked Major Powell.

The younger Indian shuffled in embarrassment. "He say — canyon swallow up white men. He say 'big river bad medicine, many men die.'"

A townsman, hired to help with the loading, gave a snort of approval. "The old man ain't no fool, Powell. Many's tried to run the river and not come back. Others gave up before they got any distance. Far's I know, ain't nobody come out the other side of that canyon alive."

"Then we'll set a record," Powell replied cheerfully. This was not the first time he had been warned that his mission was foolhardy. On his scouting trip of the previous year he had been advised by trappers and other frontiersmen against trying to conquer the Colorado. Their advice had neither frightened nor impressed him. He knew there was a great risk in trying to pilot small boats through the hazardous falls and rapids of the canyons, but however dangerous it proved to be, he was convinced he could do it.

"I shall not fail," he told himself, looking at the solid boats he had so painstakingly designed. He had arranged for their construction by a reputable Chicago shipyard and had ordered their delivery by railway freight to Green River City, the station

nearest his point of departure.

Three of the boats were twenty-one feet long, built of oak with double ribbing and re-inforced stem and stern posts. The fourth, named *Emma Dean* in honor of his wife, was smaller and lighter. Just sixteen feet long and built of pine for fast rowing, it was the boat the major had chosen for his own use.

The sun was already well up in the sky on that twenty-fourth day of May. John Wesley Powell was eager to get started but he was too careful a man to endanger himself and his crew of nine by thoughtless haste. He ran a final methodical check of the loading procedure to make certain each boat carried a portion of the provisions, and that important instruments — his barometers, chronometers, sextants and watches — were stowed in water-tight compartments. Finally there was nothing left on the river bank and the men stood by their boats, waiting for the order to shove off. "All right!"

Powell called out. "Run up the flag. Here we go!"

"Good luck! Hope you make it!" called the few townspeople who had come down to watch the departure. The two Indians watched silently as the major waved to them before boarding the *Emma Dean.*

Jack Sumner and William H. Dunn pushed the boat into the water and scrambled in with their leader. The swift current caught them. The *Kitty Clyde's Sister* followed with Walter H. Powell and G. Y. Bradley aboard. O. G. Howland and his brother, Seneca, along with Frank Goodman, manned the *No Name,* while W. R. Hawkins, the expedition cook, and a Scottish boy, nineteen-year-old Andrew Hall, cast off last in the *Maid of the Canyon.*

The crew had varied backgrounds. Goodman was an Englishman who had never traveled in the western territories. Dunn, a former trapper, knew the frontier well. Sumner, Bradley, and Captain Walter Powell had served in the Civil War where Major Powell had lost his arm just above the elbow.

The water was fast and deep. The heavily loaded boats were swept downstream at a speed that tested the steersmen's skills. Green River City, the townsmen, and the Indians soon faded from view.

With the nerve-wracking moment of departure behind them, the oarsmen relaxed and, caught off-guard, their first misadventure befell them. The boats ran aground on a hidden sandbar. "Lighten the loads," called Major Powell. The men jumped out and pushed their crafts back into the current. Within the next mile one of the *Emma Dean's* oars caught on an undetected rock and snapped. Soon thereafter the river snatched oars from two of the following boats, but the crewmen recovered them.

Now they were face to face with the wilderness — the mighty, unpredictable, unexplored wilderness. It was up to them to take care of themselves and meet all emergencies. No help could be expected. There were no ranches, towns, or settlements for a thousand miles. The ten men and their small boats were in a world of their own.

Perhaps to cheer his party, or to calm his own anxieties, Powell began to sing. He had a strong, pleasant voice and the men soon joined in, their voices rising above the roar of the river.

As the morning passed the sun's heat and glare

began to tire the crews. They welcomed the major's signal to beach their boats near a grove of cotton-woods, where new green leaves shimmered in the sunlight. After this first workout on the water it was good to stand on firm ground. The men were hungry and Hawkins did not have to call twice to bring everyone to the campfire, where coffee was boiling and the air was filled with the aroma of frying bacon.

They fought the river through the long after-noon and that night they made camp in the shelter of an overhanging cliff. Major Powell, who seemed to have the energy of six men, climbed up through a crevice to reconnoiter. Strangely eroded rocks stood out in the evening sunlight in vari-colored beauty. The buttes that had provided such a spectacular backdrop for Green River City had been a rich red, but here their pastel shades were enhanced by the setting sun. Powell recorded his impressions in his diary, noting the "witchery of light and shadow." He could see the Uinta Moun-tains far off in the distance, snow glittering on their high peaks and rosy clouds hovering above them.

After a still, clear night, the Powell party awoke to an overcast dawn. As they moved downriver a heavy rain thoroughly drenched them before they found another suitable camping spot. Once off the water they hurriedly built a roaring fire. Freshly boiled coffee restored their spirits while their clothing and supplies dried. When the sky cleared, one of the men trailed a little band of mountain sheep, and the fat lamb he brought back made a hearty meal.

There was no talk of worry or regret. Each one was aware that he was among the very few white men ever to visit the Colorado Plateau, let alone attempt to take boats through the treacherous Grand Canyon. Old Jim Bridger, an experienced mountain man, had crossed parts of the plateau and had known the Indians of the area quite well. John Charles Frémont had made perilous explorations through some of the territory, and General William Henry Ashley had visited parts of it, much to his regret. No one had ever accomplished the 2,000-mile journey.

Powell discounted the failures of Ashley and others. For two years he had been preparing for this expedition by making geological studies of the terrain that led into the Colorado River. The more he had seen of the high plateaus and deep canyons, the more determined he had become to explore the whole system thoroughly.

Wherever he wandered he found fossils that held secrets of the country's ancient past. The Indians with their strange legends and languages fascinated him. "One could spend a lifetime here and still not learn all there is to know about this land," he wrote.

Major Powell, however, had a special reason for wanting to learn all he could. He hoped to advance the United States Government's plans for territorial settlement. "Someday, maybe soon," he told his men one night as they sat around the campfire, "families will be pushing west, seeking homesites in this very area. We must explore routes for them or they'll die by the hundreds because they'll know nothing of the trials in store for them. What we discover on this trip may be a great help to future settlers."

Few of Powell's companions shared his high ideals. They weren't thinking of the trip as a service to their country. They had been hired to do this job and they would do it to the best of their abilities, but the romance of the undertaking did not have the same appeal to them as it did to the sensitive mind of John Wesley Powell.

So far the journey had pleased him. He had

not expected it to be without some unpleasantness and it encouraged him to find the men cheerful and looking forward to being part of the first expedition to run the fearful Colorado. They were young and sturdy, used to harsh weather and the rigorous physical activity Powell demanded of himself. He could depend on them for support and he knew they looked to him for strength and intelligent leadership.

On the more placid stretches of the river, they marveled at the bordering cliffs that sometimes towered over them to heights of a thousand feet. As they looked up side canyons they frequently found unexpected meadows where deer browsed. Geese and ducks were plentiful, providing fresh meat for evening meals.

During his explorations the year before, Major Powell had left a chronometer, some barometer tubes, a sextant, and other items in a cache at the junction of Henry's Fork with the Colorado. When he spied the cave where the equipment had been hidden, he could scarcely contain his anxiety. Had it been discovered and stolen? Had Indians taken the chronometer wheels for hair ornaments and the barometer tubes for beads? Happily, his fears were groundless. Everything was as he had left it.

He stowed the instruments in his boat and continued on the journey.

Powell had been warned about a gorge not far from the mouth of Henry's Fork. Suddenly, his boats were swept into it. Fiery-hued cliffs narrowed to walls over a thousand feet high. He immediately named it *Flaming Gorge*. Through this deep gash in the earth the river ran like a wild stallion, bucking and twisting over murderously sharp rocks that were hidden in a froth of white foam.

The little boats hit these waters with a shuddering impact. The oarsmen tightened their grips and gave their total energies to navigating. Engulfed by the torrent, they ran between the rocks that could have crushed the boats to matchsticks. A blur of wild motion — one final thrust — and they were through! Men and boats had been equal to the challenge.

On the other side they found smoother waters that ran through a little valley. Here they made camp and basked in their accomplishment, quietly discussing the episode. Shooting the rapids of Flaming Gorge had been their first great victory in what was to become one of the most incredible struggles in recorded exploration.

2

Looking Backward

WHAT FORCES DROVE John Wesley Powell to attempt such an impossible journey? The events of his past had undoubtedly shaped his ambitions and given him the hardihood and self-assurance he would need for this undertaking.

He was the oldest child of a stern Wesleyan minister who never stayed long in one place. His gentle mother, Mary, had borne seven more children — Bram and Walter, Mary, Martha, Lida,

Nell and Juliet. There had never been quite enough of anything — food, clothing, warmth, or attention — to go around.

Wes, as he was called by his family and close friends, did not resent any lack of pampering. He performed the many chores allotted to him without feeling abused and still found time to go adventuring in the woods and along the rivers. With his friends he spent hours swimming and sailing in rough homemade boats. He learned to caulk these boats and to bail them out when they leaked. It was all a part of the fun of growing up and he had no idea how valuable this experience would prove later.

During his early schooldays in the small but growing town of Jackson, Ohio, he was attacked by local bullies. They threw stones at him and his brother, Walter, calling them vile names because the Reverend Mr. Powell was among a growing number of people who wanted Congress to outlaw slavery in the South. To be an Abolitionist, as the advocates of freedom for the Negro were called, was disgraceful to those who upheld slavery, and there were many who did, even in that northern state.

The ruffians grew bolder when the Powell children did not fight back. Soon Wes and Walter were returning from school each day covered with blood and bruises.

"Just don't show the white feather," their father commanded. "They'll give up when they see you aren't going to run from them."

"Yes, sir," Wes mumbled through bleeding lips, "but those stones hurt pretty bad. Wouldn't it be all right for us to give them back some of their own?"

"Violence is not the answer," his father replied. "Forgive them, and show them that might does not make right."

"Yes, Father," Wes answered dutifully. He did not agree with this philosophy, but because he had a great deal of endurance, and an even greater respect for his father's anger at any resistance to his orders, he obeyed. He and Walter might have gone on being beaten and called names indefinitely except for a giant of a man named George Crookham.

Crookham interfered one day during an unequal battle where Wes was doing his best to protect his younger brother while at the same time dodging a barrage of rocks and stones that his

torturers were flinging his way.

"Git!" Crookham roared at the attackers. "Leave these lads alone or I'll tan your hides in short order." As he got down from his wagon, the gang took one look at his size and scattered.

Crookham took Wes and his brother home and spoke firmly to Preacher Powell. "You've got bright boys here. There's no sense in having them beaten and stoned every day just because you, like me, favor abolition of slavery. How do you think they'll ever learn anything this way? Let them come to my house and I'll teach them things they need to know."

"I won't have my sons acting like cowards," the Reverend Powell declared. "They must stand up to life. But neither will I have them raise their hands in violence."

"Do you want them killed?" Crookham thundered. "Or their eyes put out by a stray rock? Sir! Let your sons grow to manhood in decency."

"I think he's right, Joseph," Mrs. Powell murmured. "Let them go with Mr. Crookham. I'm heartsick at the sight of them bloody and crying."

Wes loved Crookham's approach to learning. "Take a look around," he ordered. "What do you see? . . . Look again! . . . Now, what do you see?" He was never satisfied until the boy took in all the details of the landscape, the river, the load of corn, or whatever they were observing. It became a wonderful game — seeing in depth — and it intensified Powell's fascination with the world around him.

As his range of knowledge grew, so did his perception. He began to see beyond the surface of things to their inner meanings. He learned the movements of the planets and constellations. He memorized the names of hundreds of plants and flowers and amassed a large botanical collection. His studies of the earth's development led him to searches along sharply carved river banks where he excitedly discovered fossilized rocks and shells, marking the former presence of the great seas that had covered the land.

One of the famous men of the area was William Mather, a geologist and professor of natural science. He was a friend of Crookham, and Wes was often invited to join them on extensive hikes through the country. Their conversations and observations opened a new world for this bright young boy. Each visit with the vital, well-educated Mr. Mather deepened his interest in geology.

When Crookham took him to see Mather's mineralogical specimens, Wes was awed by the tremendous extent and variety of the collection. As he tried desperately to remember every rock and crystal by name, he decided he was going to be a geologist. The earth called to him, "Come search me out. See my treasures. Sample them. Take what you will. There is so much for you to learn."

Then his restless father moved from Ohio. He wanted to rear his large family on a farm. Wisconsin seemed the ideal place. The land was rich and he would leave the abolitionist wrangles behind him. His boys, especially twelve-year-old Wes, could help him work the land.

John Wesley Powell admired the beauty of this new frontier country but the work was hard for a youngster. He was glad when his father's restlessness brought another move, this time to Bonus Prairie, Illinois. Once the family was settled Wes was free to find a job for himself. He was eighteen and on his own.

That summer he worked on barges and steamboats plying the Mississippi and Missouri rivers. Strong young men were in demand, and the experience he gained on these trips laid the foundations for his future.

Wes Powell's desire to explore books was as great as his enthusiasm for the countryside and rivers. It had been his task, on the Wisconsin farm, to haul grain to market. The trips were long and boring until he thought to take a book or two with him. As the wagon lumbered slowly along he sat lost in the printed pages. Without realizing what he was doing, he was educating himself.

He had dreamed of a college education, and for a while this looked possible with his father's help. But at the crucial moment they clashed. "You will, of course, follow in my footsteps," Reverend Powell said. "I mean, you do intend to become a minister of God, do you not?"

"No, Father," Wes replied. "I'm not cut out for a preacher. I want to be a scientist. That is what I intend to study."

His father's disappointment made him stubborn and angry. "Then you'll have no help from me," he declared, and Mrs. Powell's gentle persuasion could not sway him.

"It's because of that George Crookham . . . and that geologist, William Mather," the minister told her. "I should never have allowed him to study with those men. Science, Bah! Hard telling what mischief they poured into his young head."

Wes was tempted to argue the point with his father, but he knew it was useless. Mention of those names, however, turned his thoughts back to the wonder-days of his childhood. He felt profound gratitude toward the two men who had opened his mind to so many courses of thought and action. One of the saddest days in his young life had been when the anti-abolitionists burned George Crookham's house and his private museum with its thousands of carefully indexed specimens. Remembering these remarkable men, he vowed to get a college education — somehow!

In those days very little formal learning was needed to get a job teaching school. Wes had always had an intellectual advantage from being trained in the fluent English of his father, both at home and in the pulpit. He was a good speaker himself, and as the weather grew colder and river work slackened, he decided to hire out as a country school teacher.

Like his own tutors, Crookham and Mather, Wes Powell was an unusual teacher for his time. He did not depend on the rote learning presented by the rather dull textbooks of the day. "My aim is to teach you to see the wonders all about you — the earth in all its varieties. We'll look at Nature and her marvels of seed and flower and search for signs that point to the past — like fossils and Indian artifacts. After that we'll come back to routine book learning, just for a change . . . and to please the school board!" he told his pupils. They delighted in his methods. It was great sport to go hiking on an autumn afternoon with such a guide as Powell.

He was learning right along with them. At night, after his family had gone to bed, he poured over his books, many of them given to him back in Ohio by George Crookham and William Mather. He concentrated on the study of geology. The erosion of the land from wind and water, the actions of volcanoes and earthquakes intrigued him.

Always in the back of his mind was the idea that he must learn more about the country's first residents, the American Indians. His concern for them had begun when, as a young boy, he accompanied Crookham and Mather to one of the huge mounds in Ohio. He had listened eagerly as they speculated on the Indians' reasons for erecting the great earthworks. He had found a spearpoint there, so beautifully worked that Mather offered him a good sum of money for it. Young Powell had declined the offer and given the specimen to Mather for preservation among his collection of artifacts.

After he had been teaching for some time, his father helped organize the Illinois Institute and Wes enrolled as a student. The school offered no science courses and he soon left for Jacksonville,

Illinois, where Illinois College seemed to promise more opportunities in his chosen field. But that small school did not meet the challenges of his active mind, so he dropped out to go on a collecting trip across Wisconsin, reveling in the outdoor life.

Since childhood he had been interested in fossils and shells. He had a prize-winning mollusk collection of which he was justly proud. He had taught himself higher mathematics, knowing this would be necessary for making the accurate measurements required of scientists. He had learned to maneuver a boat with great skill and had taken one long journey alone in a skiff, riding the Mississippi to New Orleans. For a small-town boy and the son of a preacher who had never accumulated worldly goods, Wes Powell had gone a long way and had learned many things that would help him in later life.

He was a restless young man, resembling his father in that trait. A good school teacher, who worked creatively to stimulate his students, he was eventually named principal of the Hennepin, Illinois public schools. During the summers he lectured on geology and geography, traveling on a lyceum circuit through many of the adjacent states. These educational tent shows and lectures were important forms of information and entertainment for the inhabitants of small midwestern towns. He spent all his spare time on the trips studying the land and collecting specimens of minerals, shells and artifacts.

When he went with his mother to a family reunion in Detroit, Michigan, he met his cousin, Emma Dean. They were immediately attracted to each other because they held so many interests in common. Emma was a hardy girl who went hiking with Wes and helped him collect all sorts of specimens, including snakes. He fell in love with her despite objections from both families. At that time he did not have enough money to marry her and set up a household, but they wrote long, devoted letters and vowed to marry eventually.

The Civil War, so long a threat, became an actuality. John Wesley Powell was one of the first to offer his services to the cause of the North. He enlisted in the Union Army on April 14, 1861, at the age of twenty-seven, and threw himself into the training program with such fervor that by June he was named lieutenant. In November he was promoted to the rank of captain.

He determined that Emma should become his wife at once. During a leave he married her and brought her back to his post at Cape Girardeau, Missouri. Luck stayed with him until the Battle of Shiloh. There, as he raised his right arm to give a firing signal, a bullet ripped through his hand and slanted upward. Many of his dreams seemed to be shattered along with his strong forearm. Infection set in, and the arm had to be amputated above the elbow.

But Powell was not one to relinquish his dreams without a struggle. As soon as his wound healed, he returned to the army and was given an artillery command. His younger brother, Walter, was in his battery. Both men survived the terrible War Between the States, but Walter was captured and imprisoned in Atlanta where he suffered a temporary mental breakdown. The brothers were little more than walking skeletons when they returned home, Wes as a major and Walter as a captain.

After the rigors of war a new life began for Wes Powell and his wife. He was appointed professor of geology at Illinois Wesleyan University in

Bloomington. Soon he organized the first chapter of the State Natural History Society in the hope that people would learn more of the past and present wonders of their country.

His career moved steadily forward. He managed to secure a grant for a museum to be built in connection with the Natural History Society. This grant enabled the Society to hire a curator, and Powell was named to this post.

He had long considered the idea of an expedition to the unmapped wilderness of the West. In his new position, he requested government funds to help finance such a journey. Thanks to the assistance of his old army commander, Ulysses S. Grant, now president of the United States, he received the money.

In the summer of 1867, Emma Dean Powell, riding a pinto pony, was one of a party of explorers, led by her husband, who climbed the Rockies in Colorado. She became the first white woman to climb Pikes Peak and handled the trip as competently as her companions. The whole party suffered from the wind and cold and snow at that high altitude.

On this journey nothing escaped the trained

eye of John Wesley Powell. Enchanted by his surroundings, he made extensive notes and sketches to fix the changing scene in his mind. He observed how each brook formed its own small canyon through the rocky terrain, and how the rivers gathered force as they rushed forward, lashing the land they invaded and all the while creating a fearful music of wave and spray. He saw long lines of colored cliffs and the protruding blackness of lava plugs that told of eruptions and earthquakes which had caused the faults in the earth so often found in the West. He was touched by the efforts of primitive men to create a life in a bleak country where whatever comfort they enjoyed had to be hued out of the rocks and cinders and soil.

Emma Dean Powell understood and encouraged her husband's ambition to challenge the unknown. After he and his men had climbed Longs Peak, and he had looked down into the emerald green water of Grand Lake, the headland of the Colorado River, Powell told her he would never rest until he had gone the whole way along that river and through the dark vastness of the Grand Canyon.

3

Disaster Falls

Now that journey had begun! They had been on the river for five days and had traveled 75 miles. The wilderness deepened as they moved southward from Flaming Gorge. Occasionally a grizzly bear reared on hind legs to stare at them from the river's edge. Elk grazed unperturbed in grassy spots. Side canyons often revealed small bands of mountain sheep or mule deer as well as bobcats and wolverines.

The birds were particularly engaging. In one canyon thousands of swallows twittered and swooped, snatching up beakfuls of mud from the banks of a stream and carrying it to the cliffs where they daubed it against the rocks to build houses for their families-to-be. Kingfishers dived from crags to catch unwary fish that were swimming in the cold, clear water. A variety of song birds enriched the still mornings.

Major Powell, in the *Emma Dean*, was setting a strong pace when he heard an ominous roar. He immediately signalled the following boatsmen to make for the river bank and tie up. "Falls beyond!"

That warning meant the end of leisurely travel for awhile. It would be necessary to perform a "let down" as the men called it. The boats had to be unloaded and lowered on ropes into safe waters below the falls. Then the supplies had to be carried down on foot. There was no other way to proceed with safety.

By the time all four boats had been lowered and secured, the men were exhausted. A night's rest restored them and they were threading their way among the rocks, burdened with provisions, when they saw a name and a date painted on a cliff wall. "Ashley, 1825!" Major Powell exclaimed. "So he got this far!"

Probably the name had been painted on the cliff by General William Henry Ashley, a Virginian who had become the first governor of the state of Missouri in 1820, but who had not been able to resist the lure of the western wilderness. His interest had involved him in the fur trapping industry, and after a trappers' meeting in that area he tried running the Green River, nearly losing his life in the endeavor. His crudely-made buffalo skin boats had capsized and only one of the trappers in his party survived with him. Their provisions were lost to the river and for six days they had wandered along canyon walls, which they could not climb. They were found by a French trapper named Etienne Provo, who gave them food and helped them reach a Mormon settlement. After this experience Ashley had sold his trapping interests and returned to the East where he became a Congressman.

The Powell party found remnants of one of Ashley's wrecked boats and scattered pots and pans that had, no doubt, been washed onto the shore after the disaster. Careful scouting produced no further revelations, however, and they set forth again, hoping for smoother waters. This was not to be. They soon reached another canyon of towering walls where they heard a roar intensified by echoes. The river plunged over half-hidden rocks, and Powell knew they were in danger of being washed overboard by the tremendously high waves.

He had told his men to cling to the boats, should they be swept out or capsized, because the waterproofed compartments would keep them from sinking. Since it was late in the day, he signalled the party to shore, putting off any attempt to run the rapids ahead until the following morning.

By this time it was June. The nights were warmer, and the stars shone brightly in the dark sky above the campsite. There was nothing but the thought of the next day's danger and the roar of the rapids to disturb their rest. One of the men, remembering a poem he had read, suggested that the major name this canyon after it. Powell, who also recalled the poem, marked *The Canyon of Lodore* on his map.

For a long time that night Major Powell lay

awake watching the slow wheeling of the stars in the heavens and wondering how he might best bring his group to safety through those roiling waters that seemed to roar even more menacingly in the quiet of the night.

With the first light of day he left camp to climb to a vantage point where he could assess the risks involved. "There's one quiet stretch," he reported, "where I think we can row across to a landing place, if we're careful. I'll lead the way."

He made the crossing safely. With the *Emma Dean* secured, he handed the signal flag to one of his companions. "Guide the others across," he said, "while I take a look at the next turn."

After he watched the safe passage and landing of the *Kitty Clyde's Sister*, Powell began his climb up a cliff. Soon a shout startled him. Someone was in trouble. He paused on a narrow ledge and looked back.

It was the *No Name*. It had been swept into the leaping waves of the rapids and was plunging toward the falls. From his ledge, the major could see that the boat was certain to go over. With a sinking heart he began his descent, now hoping only to save the fourth boat, *Maid of the Canyon*, which he feared would follow the course of the *No Name*. The *Maid* avoided the treacherous spots, however, and joined the other two boats at the landing.

But what of the *No Name* and her passengers? Scrambling over the rocks, Powell looked down to see the stricken boat crash into a huge rock, fly into the air, strike another rock as it came down, then break open and spill its crew into the seething water. For a moment he lost sight of it again, then he glimpsed it drifting downriver, the crew clinging to its broken parts.

The shattered pieces swirled out of sight once more, and when Major Powell sighted them again the men had abandoned their positions. Goodman was clinging to a boulder, the waves lashing him brutally against it. Howland, who had been washed onto an island nearby, was trying to rescue him. Seneca Howland was swimming to safety.

Powell watched O. G. Howland's heroic attempt to extend a pole to Goodman, and wondered if Goodman would be able to grasp it, even if Howland succeeded in pushing it within reaching distance. He gave a yell of encouragement as Goodman, at the risk of being swept away,

grabbed the pole and was pulled ashore. They were safe, but the *No Name* was lost.

When the crew was assembled once more, they inventoried the missing supplies and discussed what could be done to salvage part of the lost cargo. "The main thing is that the crew is alive and unhurt," Major Powell said. "It would be dangerous to try to reach the wreck."

He was sincere in his desire to protect his men, but there was another problem — the two barometers he needed so badly were in the cabin of the ruined boat. The loss of some of the provisions was serious, but they could do without them. However, it would be impossible to obtain more barometers. Powell slept very little that night.

By morning he had decided he must try to recover these devices that were so important to the success of the exploration. If the barometers were still in the cabin, and if the cabin section of the boat had by luck remained lodged between some rocks where he had last seen it, there was a chance that the instruments might be found in working condition.

He had a bad moment when he discovered that the cabin had been washed away, but it was soon spotted a short distance downstream. Sumner and Dunn volunteered to attempt the recovery.

The rest of the crew took up the arduous task of unloading the boats, letting them down over the falls, and then reloading. "We should have brought a donkey to do this work," one of the men panted. "I never realized how heavy a sack of flour could be."

Transferring the cargo kept them busy all day. A cheer went up when Sumner and Dunn reported back. They had reached the wreck and salvaged the barometers intact.

"There'll be more portages and more falls," Powell admitted, "but I hope there'll be no more losses." In remembrance of the episode he named the place *Disaster Falls*.

4

Longjohns to the Rescue

DURING THE NEXT FEW DAYS the descent of the
Green River was routine. Major Powell was
pleased with the results of his investigations. The
maps he drew, after harrowing climbs and exhausting hikes, would be invaluable to the government
agencies concerned with development of the West
and its water resources.

The wild beauty of the canyons thrilled him.
At one point he climbed a cliff that rose half a mile.

Looking down from its flat summit, he saw a sheltered grassland 800 feet below. A stream meandered through this meadow and cascaded over a ledge, making a thousand-foot fall to the river. On another excursion he came upon an enormous natural amphitheater in a cliff face. Delicate ferns grew thick on its floor. If other people had been there before him, they had left no hint of their presence.

During mid-day breaks he led various members of his party up to the surrounding plateaus. The clear summer sunlight reflected spectacularly on brightly-hued cliff walls. Powell loved the earth as few men do. Each side canyon and hidden mountain park, the pine forests of the higher elevations, and the wild animals that lived among the rocks and trees and tumbling streams were, for him, revelations of earth's rich life. It gave him pleasure to pass on his discoveries to others and to share with them the excitement of seeing this virgin landscape, so far removed from the ordinary experiences of man.

Most of the time, however, all hands were kept busy with the never-ending task of lowering the boats over the falls and rapids that faced them through a large part of their journey. Danger was never more than a breath away, as they discovered on June 16, only a week after the Disaster Falls incident.

They came to the head of a particularly hazardous falls and started work on the inevitable portage. The first two boats were lowered without trouble, but when the *Maid of the Canyon* was almost safe in the water, an eddy caught her, tearing her from the grasp of her handlers and sending her hurtling downstream through what Powell called *Hell's Half Mile.*

The cry, "She's lost!" went up. For several minutes the men looked on in helpless despair, but suddenly the little craft began spinning in a whirlpool. Crewmen manned the *Emma Dean* and maneuvered close enough to rescue the runaway.

Late that afternoon, after the boats had been run onto the sand of a little cove and preparations for the night were under way, Major Powell decided to take a hike before dusk. Below him, as he climbed, the oarsmen rested, talking about the events of the day. A campfire had been started, and young Hall was gathering armfuls of deadwood to keep it going. That they were in a dangerous location had not occurred to any of them. The stand of cedars and willows had afforded shade and wood. It seemed ideal.

Suddenly a whirlwind blew into the cove, swirling sparks and embers from the fire into the dry foliage of the cedars. Instantly the entire camping area was ablaze. Flames swept high onto the cliffs. There was no place for the men to go except the river. They ran. Hawkins snatched a load of cooking utensils, only to trip and fall at the river's edge. Pots and pans, tin plates and skillets flew into the water and were quickly carried away.

The only safety lay in the boats. The men rushed to them, cast off and rowed away from the conflagration. Bradley's ears were scorched, and the others had burned spots on their clothing, but at least they had saved themselves and the boats.

As the fire struck, Major Powell was at a point high above the camp serenely surveying the landscape. When he saw his party moving downstream, he hastily descended and ran to the place where that boats were being brought in to a new landing.

"We got burned out," his brother shouted to him. "Let's see what we can salvage." There was very little. The hot flames had been destructive.

From the unpacked supplies only a few cups, a kettle, and some bedding had escaped the blaze. Day by day, the expedition was being stripped of its meager comforts and necessities.

Just beyond the mouth of the Yampa River, which feeds into the Green River from the east, they found cliffs that echoed their words in gentle tones. The men tried to out-do one another in their calls which wafted hauntingly back to them. Major Powell was amused at the antics of a band of mountain sheep. As he climbed a crag into their territory, they stood watching him for some time before the leader, a large ram, stamped with one foot as a signal for the ewes and lambs to take flight. Then he followed, leaping among the rocks and shepherding his charges out of sight.

Powell decided to camp in the Yampa area in order to make astronomical calculations. One day he and Bradley took the *Emma Dean* a short distance upstream to look for a break in the cliffs where they could get a wider view of the stars once the clear summer nights fell.

They beached the boat under an opening that looked approachable, and Powell led the way up a cliff face carrying his barometer under the stub of his right arm. Bradley followed, carrying the barometer case. It was hard work to pick their way over the broken rocks. They had climbed well above the stream when they came to a cliff that threatened to block them completely.

The major stopped and carefully considered what action to take. In spite of having only one arm, he was an excellent climber and not a man to accept defeat. With complete confidence, he made the leap to a small foothold in the rocks and grasped a projection overhead. Then he realized his danger. He dared not let go with his left hand because there was no place for him to land. "Bradley!" he yelled. "Help me."

Bradley understood the major's predicament. "Hang on!" he shouted. "I've got to get up above you."

Major Powell was standing on his toes, his good arm stretched above his head. Already his muscles, strong though they were, ached with the strain. He knew he would not be able to maintain his position very long, and the cleft on which he was so precariously perched was more than sixty feet above the only other rock ledge in his path. Besides, if he let go and by some miracle fell uninjured, there was still the danger of rolling off the ledge and being hurled down the cliff onto the jumbled rocks. He was as close to death as Goodman had been in the river.

Bradley somehow hoisted himself up the face of the cliff and reached a narrow shelf above Powell. He looked around for something he could let down to his stranded leader, but there was nothing — not a tree limb, not a dried branch or wind-deposited pole of any sort.

"How about the barometer case?" he called. "Do you think you could grab it?"

"No," the major groaned. "Think of something else, man! And hurry."

Suddenly Bradley had an idea. It was a strange one, but it just might work. He began undressing. Off came his shoes, his pants, and his long underwear. Tying a knot in one leg and holding firmly to the other, he lowered the longjohns.

Powell's strength was ebbing. Desperately he pressed himself against the cliff face, released his slipping handhold, and grabbed the dangling leg of Bradley's drawers. Surprisingly, he still held the barometer under his right arm. After a moment's rest on Bradley's shelf, he resumed the climb, finding new accesses to the top of the cliff.

Once on safe footing, he began his scientific calculations as though nothing of importance had happened. He informed Bradley in a very matter-of-fact tone that he intended to climb Mt. Dawes the following day.

"At this elevation," he said, "and in this clear air, I should be able to see a hundred miles or more. I hope to locate the Wind River Mountains where the Green River heads. Maybe I'll see the Wasatch Range — and even the far slopes of the Rockies."

He suffered no mishaps on the next day's climb and, as he predicted, he was able to see fantastic distances in all directions. The panoramic view helped him immeasurably in charting the area. On his return he fired his rifle to assure the men below that he would soon be with them. When he entered camp, tired and hungry, he was delighted to find that some of the crew had spent the day fishing and that Hawkins had fried a panful of trout especially for him.

5

Bradley's Turn

AT EVERY TURN THE river challenged the skill and endurance of Powell and his men. Some of its canyons were narrow with almost vertical walls. Others flared out with sloping faces opposite overhanging cliffs. In places the water boiled in a seething white froth, then quieted to lake-like smoothness. Nothing could be determined in advance, except by close scouting from the crags and pinnacles above.

Major Powell had studied part of this area on his previous exploration of the land, but the river, with its whirlpools, rapids, and plunging falls, presented new problems. Entire days were spent in lowering the boats over precipices, carrying the dwindling supplies down treacherous trails, and then reloading them.

On June 24, one month after leaving Green River City near the southwestern border of Wyoming, they had traveled only a short distance southward into Utah because of the many twists and turns of the river.

Whenever Powell explored on foot he found remarkable stone formations carved out by nature. One day, however, he came upon a pile of rocks that was obviously man-made. A heavy growth of plants and lichens indicated that the work had been done many years before. The rocks bore no writing, but Major Powell believed the mound had been built by Father Silvestre Veléz de Escalante, a Franciscan priest, who headed an expedition into the area in 1776. Escalante's party had crossed the Colorado River at a point that Powell wanted to discover.

It was little wonder that so few men had attempted to travel this route since the Escalante voyage nearly a hundred years before. As the Powell party moved southward, the extraordinary courage, strength, and daring of these young men made the difference between success and disaster. Their physical stamina and determination over-came the perils of getting through surging rapids and crashing falls, of making brutal land passages over craggy rocks and across deep crevasses. Each mile was gained by unremitting toil and unusual bravery.

As the days wore on, the men grew increasingly

weary from their struggles with the churning waters. They needed a rest, and they were soon to have one. After a particularly exhausting run, the boats broke into a stretch where the river quieted into purring tranquility. They were in the heart of a beautiful mountain valley.

"Indians have camped here," Major Powell observed, pointing to tepee poles and fire pits. "Hunting party, probably. I saw a band of antelope feeding over near the cliffs. We must be near the mouth of the Uinta River. That means we aren't more than forty miles or so from the Uinta Indian Agency. I'll make a trip over there. Maybe we can get fresh supplies and send letters home. Our people will be wondering what's become of us. This spot will be our home for a few days. I have more astronomical work to do."

They camped under an old cottonwood tree. Powell told his men that this was the place where Captain E. L. Berthoud — for whom Colorado's Berthoud Pass is named — maintained headquarters while he and his crew surveyed a stage route from Salt Lake City to Denver. At this site they had built a ferry, opened a road, and crossed the Green River.

After he had finished his scientific observations, Major Powell and two of his men set out for the Ute Reservation Agency. They had hoped to go up the Uinta River by boat part of the way, but found this too difficult. The overland trek was almost as hard. The river had a way of wandering back and forth over their route, making it necessary for them to wade it several times, and at least half of the forty-mile hike was across a sandy desert. They started early in the morning and reached the Indian agent's headquarters just before dark. The agency buildings reminded them of how far removed they had been from any signs of civilization.

"It's mighty nice to see houses again," one of the men exclaimed. "Even if they're not much more than shacks and Injuns live in some of them."

"I'm glad there are Indians living here," Major Powell declared. "It gives me a chance to learn more about them."

In the morning Powell asked where Chief Tsauwiat lived and then strolled over to visit him. The chief was rumored to be nearly a hundred years old, and looked it. He was incredibly shriveled and his speech was barely understandable.

His wife was quite different. Obviously pleased to see the major, she talked eagerly about the problems of her people. "Help them learn to live like the white man lives," she begged. "Show them how to farm and grow good food."

Powell took time to visit the few irrigated plots of ground the Utes were farming. Very rarely were Indians given irrigated land. He also stopped at some of their lodges. Many of the Indians preferred these skin-covered hutches to the log cabins and frame houses of the white man. One of their objections to a fixed residence was that it could not be moved to a clean spot when dirty, nor could it be burned if someone had died in it.

Major Powell was moved by the plight of the Indians. Their poverty was pitiful. Before the coming of the white man they had lived in dignity within their own cultures. Now, pushed back onto desolate reservations and dependent upon the indifference of governmental management, they had nothing but a marginal existence.

"Something must be done for these people," Powell told the Indian agent. "We took their land and we should offer them a better life in return. They ask so little. Maybe I can help more if I learn their language. I'm going to start today."

This was the beginning of his intensive study of the various dialects of the American Indian. To him, Indians were not thieving savages, as many judged them, but people who had lost the fight for their own land and were having a bad time adjusting to a new way of life.

Examination of the foundations of ancient dwellings in the vicinity of the agency convinced Powell that the Indians who had long ago roamed those valleys had developed a much higher civilization than that of the present residents. Writings on the crumbling walls indicated that the "Old Ones" had perfected a method of communication that had been lost in time. The Utes only shook their heads when he asked about the ancient people and their language. They knew nothing of either.

Powell realized that the great valleys and the magnificent plateaus in this Utah territory would soon become known to the world. Adventurous families would start the long trek westward. There would be no holding them back. The promise of free, virgin land awaiting their plows would be too great a lure. He felt that the government should prepare for their arrival, and at the same time consider its effect upon the Utes.

Frank Goodman, the Englishman who had so narrowly escaped death when the *No Name* was wrecked, had accompanied the major to the Uinta Indian Agency. He had been looking dejected for several days, so Powell was not surprised when Goodman called him aside. "Major," he said, "I've decided not to go on with you. I'm sorry, but I've seen enough danger. I'm going back to civilization while I still can, and jolly glad to do it. Take my advice and give up the journey through that canyon. I'll be surprised if you make it alive. Judging by what we've been through, I'm certain the rest of the trip will be disastrous."

Major Powell took a deep breath. "You've chosen a good spot for your departure, Frank," he answered slowly. "Good luck to you. You've been a faithful member of the crew. We'll miss you."

So Goodman left them. Now there were nine men and three boats — three overloaded boats, even without the weight of the departing crewman. In spite of having lost supplies and equipment in their struggles with the river, they had never truly compensated for the loss of the *No*

Name, and now they were taking on new provisions.

For several days the expedition traveled uneventfully through a region so dry and forsaken that Powell named it *Desolation Canyon.* They stopped frequently to chart their route and make barometrical calculations. A mercurial barometer was read three times a day, and they carried aneroid barometers for work away from the river. Although portable, the aneroids were less accurate than the mercurials and were checked against them daily. In Powell's work the barometers were used to ascertain the height of ascent. They were most valuable in topographic mapping.

This expedition was John Wesley Powell's own private venture, but it was assisted by funds from several educational institutions, and rations were provided through the United States Government. In recompense for their support Major Powell made many notes and measurements regarding the course of the river, the altitude of the cliffs and plateaus, the geology and geography of the system, and the time consumed between points. His backers would be more than repaid by his work.

With the arrival of summer, the days grew long

and hot. Suddenly, after quiet passages, danger lurked around one of the abrupt curves of the canyon. In running a rapid the pilot boat, *Emma Dean*, lost one oar and broke another. A new rapid loomed ahead. Powell had to make a quick decision. "I think we can do it," he reported to the men at the remaining oars, but as he neared the rapid and saw the peril of their position, he shouted, "No, no! Bring her to shore!"

The swiftness of the water made it impossible to carry out his order. The *Emma Dean* shot downstream even as the major signalled the other boats to land if they could. It was hurtling forward when a wave hit, swamping it. Another wave crested, and over it went!

Powell was thrown clear and immediately began swimming. As the waves rolled over him he caught a glimpse of the boat floating ahead with Jack Sumner and William Dunn clinging to it. He reached them, and the three men hung on until they reached a stretch of quieter water. There they righted the boat but almost lost Dunn when his hold slipped. He had to be hauled back by Sumner.

Hearing the roar of another rapid ahead and not knowing how treacherous it might be, they swam for shore, towing the boat with them. Major Powell caught a bundle drifting past. It was a roll of blankets that had fallen from the capsized boat. Unfortunately, a barometer, two guns, and other blanket rolls had disappeared in the swift waters. Once in camp they dried their clothing and remaining blankets over a driftwood fire. The rest of the day was spent in converting other pieces of driftwood into oars.

Back on the water they were almost through Desolation Canyon when a wave swept over the *Kitty Clyde's Sister,* knocking Bradley overboard. It would have carried him downstream but his foot caught beneath the seat. For a terrifying moment he was pulled forward, his head under water. Then he managed to grab the side of the boat and lift his face from the waves long enough to get a breath of air.

Major Powell, whose boat had gone through the rough water safely, looked back helplessly while it appeared that Bradley was being dragged to his death. Any moment he could be smashed against a rock and his head crushed like an eggshell.

Captain Walter Powell was at the oars of the

Kitty Clyde. Although to the watching crewsmen it seemed that he was unaware of Bradley's danger, the coolheaded young man was merely intent on choosing the best course of action. With a few powerful sweeps of the oars, Walter Powell brought the boat into safer waters, then unceremoniously grabbed Bradley's clothing and hauled him on board. Bradley huddled there, coughing and spitting water, so relieved to be alive that he almost failed to notice his twisted ankle.

That night as they were camped on a sandy beach, another swirling wind came up. It lifted the fine sand like blowing flour and almost stifled the men. The next morning they shook piles of it from their blankets and tried unsuccessfully to comb it from their hair.

"Well," drawled Hawkins, kicking bits of driftwood together for the morning fire, "Goodman and Howland, and even the major, have had their brushes with death. Now Bradley's joined them. Who's next?" No one volunteered for that dubious honor.

9
The Dirty Devil

DRIFTED SAND DUNES on either side of the river, instead of towering cliffs, marked the expedition's emergence from the almost hundred-mile stretch of Desolation Canyon. The July sun, beating down on those long stretches of sand, seemed to set the landscape afire, and the reflected glare strained their vision. Mirages came and went. The area seemed to be in motion with the transparent quivering and shifting of heat waves.

Gray Canyon offered them refuge from the heat waves as a change of color appeared in the cliffs. The brightly-hued layers gave way to cool and soothing blue shades.

Major Powell understood the meaning of the rock layers and he spent much of his time making notes. He read the cliffs in passing as one might read a book printed in large type. Anticlines, synclines, folding, cross bedding — he used these terms to describe how the rocks had been formed during millions of years.

One afternoon Jack Sumner noticed Powell intently scanning the river banks ahead. "What you looking for, Major?" he called.

"Gunnison's Crossing," Powell replied. "We can't be far from it." They had come into a valley with cottonwood trees on both sides of a broad and peaceful stream.

"Looks like an Indian crossing," Sumner observed. "See the log raft floating over there by that little island."

"This is the place where Captain Gunnison crossed the river in 1863," the major said. "Only place it can be crossed for many miles. Gunnison was killed by Indians not long afterward. . . . Let's see what Indian signs we can find."

They found few artifacts, but the next day when they stopped at the mouth of the San Rafael River, they found Indian trails leading down to the water. Flint chips and projectile points told of leisurely campsites in the past. If any Indians still hovered in the area, they took pains to remain out of sight.

Now, instead of shooting the boats along like bullets, the water was so still that the oarsmen had to work hard to make any headway. "If it ain't one thing it's another," one of them grumbled.

Again the scenery had changed. The river cliffs were no longer pale blue but a brilliant orange. They were formed of sandstone, however, like most of the canyons on the journey.

The major climbed to a high point and on his return told the men that the river ahead writhed like a snake, turning back on itself so sharply that, as they went downstream, they would find themselves directly across from the place where they had been half an hour before.

The canyons were shorter on this stretch of the trip. Each turn of the river offered new sights, some of them awesome. At one point they saw what looked like an immense fallen cross with walls

more than two thousand feet high. They named it the *Butte of the Cross,* but later, looking down on it, they saw that it was in reality two buttes, so positioned that one lay in front of the other. Their eyes had played tricks on them.

They were constantly surrounded by rocks, grotesquely carved by wind and water. There were pinnacles and mesas and domes, some of them so rounded and scored that they might have been ground by a giant's sander. The junction of the Green River, the Grand River, and the mighty Colorado was drawing closer. After that meeting they would race into the perilous waters of the Grand Canyon itself.

Near the junction they stopped to check their supplies. They found that their bacon was moldy and rancid, but that they still had a good supply of coffee. "Our flour's been wet so many times, there's not going to be much to screen," Hawkins declared, using a piece of mosquito netting as a strainer.

They had not suffered for fresh meat. Hawkins was an excellent hunter and often brought back a deer, a lamb, or a brace of ducks. Now and then he killed a goose or came in with a good mess of fish. He had no fancy trimmings for the fowl, but the roasted meat always tasted good to the famished travelers.

They had barely set out on the Colorado River when the *Emma Dean* capsized in another rapid. Again the men were thrown out, but clung to the boat until it drifted into quieter waters where they could right it. This time they lost three oars, and there were no trees along the river to furnish material for replacements. In fact there were no sandy beaches for a camping spot. They slept that night on bare rocks.

It was dangerous to go on, but there was no choice. They were forced to continue the journey as best they could until they found timber of some sort. Fortunately it was not many miles until they saw a rock ledge where driftwood had accumulated. From the pile of debris they untangled some long branches that could be made into oars.

While the others sawed and shaped the raw timber into oars, Major Powell and his brother climbed above camp to look for cedar trees from which they could gather pitch to caulk the badly leaking boats. Checking the barometer, Major Powell told his brother, "We are at fifteen-hundred feet right here and some of the cliffs are twice that, I'm certain."

So far they had not lacked fresh drinking water, even though what they collected was sometimes cloudy from the run-off after summer storms. There was always water to be found in pools within the rocks, and if these pools were deep enough, a man could swim, or at least have a refreshing dip.

During his hikes Powell often came upon hidden glens where water trickled from springs bubbling down from a crevice in the rocks, and aromatic pines offered shade. Sometimes a narrow side canyon widened into a green pocket where tall grass grew and wild flowers bloomed in profusion.

One day, while they were still working to finish new oars and repair the damaged boats, the major and four of his party headed up one of the narrow side canyons, which widened until it became a great cave, its rock ceiling far overhead. "Back at camp," Powell said, "I noticed the high water marks on the cliffs. They were almost a hundred feet above us. We'd better keep an eye on the weather. If there was to be a cloudburst, water would run down this canyon as if it were a funnel."

Bradley agreed. "There was driftwood caught on a ledge at least fifty feet above us. But there's no sign of a storm at present."

The four crewmen scattered, intent on their own observations. Major Powell found a narrow crevice and after examining it, decided he could work his way up by bracing his knees against one side and sliding his body up inch by inch on the other. This method was working very well until the crevice widened. He could no longer brace his knees against the opposite wall and he was at least twenty-five feet above his starting point. Since he had never allowed the fact that he had only one whole arm to daunt him, he met this situation by dropping back down into the narrower portion of the crevice where he could rest for a moment. Then, finding new holds, he struggled upward, and in a few moments was on top of the cliff.

Here he smelled the sharp fragrance of pitch. There were cedar trees among the rocks and they were oozing droplets of clear pitch, stimulated by the hot sun.

"Just what we need!" the major told himself. "But what can I carry it in?" There was nothing — except his empty shirt sleeve! He whipped his hunting knife from its sheath and cut the sleeve off, then tied a knot in the small end of it. Hanging his barometer on a cedar branch, he began dipping pitch into his makeshift bag.

He was too busy with his new enterprise to notice the gathering storm clouds. When he had filled the shirtsleeve, he took his barometer and began making his customary notations. It was not until he heard a crash of thunder that he became aware of a change in the weather. When lightning sizzled among the rocks where he was standing, he grabbed the bag of pitch and dashed for shelter.

The rain broke in a sudden downpour that almost washed him off the rocks before he found the way down into a little side canyon. He knew his safety, as well as that of the men and supplies in camp, depended on how quickly he could slip and slide down to them.

He was not an instant too soon. When he reached river level and looked back he could see a flow of red mud following his recent avenue of escape. "Move out!" he shouted. "Hurry! Flash flood's coming our way." The crews lost no time in complying with his order, and as the red torrent rolled into the river, Powell realized there would be no clear water for many days. There was one happy note connected with this incident, however. Some deer had been driven down by the storm and Hawkins, always mindful of the scarcity of food, shot a fat one that made a feast for the party after the storm had passed.

"There's another stream flowing into the Colorado from the northwest," Major Powell encouraged the men when they were forced to drink from the murky stream. "Let's hope it's sweet water, with none of this mud."

"Let's hope it's a good trout stream," one of the men laughed. "Venison's good but trout's even better."

When they reached the mouth of the river Powell had mentioned, their eagerness was dispelled by the first swallow of water. "This is no trout stream," Bill Dunn stormed, after drinking a sample he had dipped up in his hand. "She's a dirty devil, this river."

The others laughed, but agreed with his description, and Powell entered the name *Dirty Devil* on his maps, giving the river's three tributaries their own fitting titles — *Stinking River, Muddy River,* and *Starvation River.*

7
Beautiful Glen Canyon

THE VOYAGERS' ROUTE provided contrasting experiences. What had been treacherous or ugly might quickly give way to surroundings of fantastic beauty. After the battle with the red mud Powell and his crew moved into the smoother waters of a magnificent canyon. Entering it unsuspectingly, they realized its grandeur little by little. Each new discovery struck them as more remarkable than the last.

For Powell, the geologist, the history of the earth lay in the banded cliffs and cross-bedded sandstone and lava projections. The rocks here had been turned into a tapestry of rainbow hues by mineral deposits in the water which poured down from above.

The boats had been drifting downriver, after running a rapid so tame in comparison to previous wild encounters that it seemed almost trivial, when the major pointed toward the canyon wall. It was broken at that point with several overhanging ledges like great steps. At the base of the lowest ledge, the facing rocks crumbled into a talus slope trailing into the river.

"House up there," he called out. "Let's have a look." The other boats followed the *Emma Dean* to a small bay in a stream that tumbled down a crevice to join the Colorado.

In his eagerness, Powell waited for no one, but immediately scrambled up ledge after ledge until he reached a great overhang where the ruins of a stone dwelling had long awaited residents who never came home.

Upon examing the construction, he was impressed by the precise way in which the rocks had

been fitted together. Judging by the amount of rubble, he speculated that there had been many rooms and perhaps three stories to the building.

Who were the dwellers in the rocks? Where had they come from and why had they left? Were they, like the westbound travelers of his time, looking for a safe home? What fear had made them seek such high shelter? Had animals, as fearsome as the dinosaurs who had left their gigantic three-toed tracks in this area, threatened them? Had they been intimidated by other tribes who had eventually overpowered them and gone on to other conquests? Had drought dried up their little river farms or had flood waters washed out their gardens and sent their plants downriver?

These ancient people had been advanced enough to make pottery. Powell found many potsherds, their decorative patterns now faded. Projectile points of flint and obsidian were strewn about. One wall-joining contained prints of a tiny corncob, plastered there, perhaps, by some Indian woman with a love of beauty. A short distance from the main ruin stood a storage hut, empty now of any traces of corn which had been carried off by packrats and chipmunks.

The quiet of the ruins stirred a deep emotion in the major. He removed his hat and sat down, staring at the mute stones and wishing they could speak of what had taken place when the now vanished people had lived in this beautiful canyon.

Returning to the riverside, he and his men found cliff walls covered with petroglyphs. These pictures, etched into the rocks by pecking at the sandstone with sharp tools, intrigued the party, although no one understood their meaning. "At least they tried to leave a record," said one of the men admiringly.

"Someday we may be able to read these pictures," Powell mused while making sketches of the rock writings in his notebook. I'd like to find the key to this area's history on these rocks — the 'Rosetta Stone' as it were." Just as in 1799, near the banks of the Nile, Napoleon's troops had found an inscribed basalt slab which was to become the key to Egyptian hieroglyphics, so Major Powell hoped that he and his little band might have come upon a code for interpreting ancient Indian communication.

"At least you're learning some of the present language of the Indians," his brother observed. This in itself was a challenging study. The guttural sounds were difficult to remember and bore no relationship to English.

"The thing that helps me," said the major, "is that they don't have very large vocabularies. There are a few key words used over and over, I'm keeping a list of the new ones I run across. For instance they call this rocky land the 'Toom-pin-tu-weap'."

The next day, as they floated downriver, they saw what looked like a trail leading up a bare sandstone rockface. Puzzled by the strange markings, they stopped to examine them. Toeholds had been laboriously pecked into the sandstone, forming a path which zigzagged up the steep cliff to the ruins of another rock house in a small cave, and from there to an exit on top.

"They may have carried their household water up from the river," the men reasoned. "And maybe, if other tribes came to make war on them, they escaped from the canyon to the mesas above." Looking at the slight anchorage the toeholds would afford, Powell shook his head in wonder. Whoever these inhabitants had been, they must have had great courage and lively, inventive minds.

"Were these your people who once lived here?" he asked a solitary Indian who appeared at their camp one day as if by magic.

The Indian shook his head. "Old Ones," he grunted and then tried to express his own beliefs about the ancients who had made the rugged canyon their home for a time. The major struggled to understand the flow of Indian words and attempted to question their visitor about the rituals of his own people.

"They have 'kivas' like the Hopi Indians," Powell told his men later. "These kivas are underground meeting places where they carry on their secret tribal ceremonies . . . something like our lodge rooms."

They had gone through canyon after canyon

in their progress down the river and now they were at the mouth of one of its great tributaries, the San Juan, whose headwaters were in the saw-toothed San Juan Mountains of Colorado just below the Continental Divide.

Officially the Colorado begins as a little trickle of melted snow 10,000 feet up in the Never Summer Mountains northwest of Denver. Its other major tributary, the Green River, rises in a stand of lodgepole pine close to the Continental Divide in Wyoming's Wind River Mountains. As the combined waters that make up the Colorado tumble toward the Pacific Ocean, they drain 240,000 square miles of country in seven states—Wyoming, Utah, Colorado, Arizona, New Mexico, Nevada and California. The system covers one-twelfth of the United States. "This is one of the most fascinating waterways on earth," Powell once declared, "and one of the longest."

The cliffs had run the whole range of colors — all the tones of yellows and reds and blues, as well as some greens, whites and blacks. Here at the merging of the San Juan with the Colorado, their hues were even more spectacular. Minerals had striated the immense walls in striking patterns as the water had flowed from the highlands.

During his land exploration, the major had noted how the San Juan twisted and turned like a snake through the Indian lands. He had looked down on this area before, but he was not prepared for the many wonders of the place as viewed from the river. He was later to name it *Glen Canyon.*

Looking to the future and the growing population of the Southwest, he could foresee the need for dams along such rivers as the Green and the Colorado. These dams would furnish irrigation for thousands of acres of dry lands in the states that bordered these rivers.

"The settlers will need food, and they cannot count on the occasional good crop from the un-irrigated land in this rainless country. They will need water in great quantities," he advised his men.

He knew the Homestead Act of 1862 would lure land-seeking pioneers to this country just as it was already bringing thousands into the prairie lands of Kansas, Nebraska, Missouri, Oklahoma, and other states once known only to roving tribes of Indians and a few adventurous frontiersmen.

He was aware, too, that Eastern politicians

knew almost nothing about the problems which frontier settlers faced. He had already framed reports that would help to solve these problems, but he was ahead of his time and few were willing to listen to him.

There was irony in Powell's exploration of Glen Canyon and his meticulous charting of its terrain. He would never know that this site was to become a tremendous memorial to him. In the next century the canyon would be turned into *Lake Powell*, contained by a great dam. The area of his observations would be flooded and lost forever in a future engineering feat, but his name would live on.

The expeditionary force was grateful for the comparatively quiet passages through Glen Canyon and its pleasant campsites. On the night of July 31, soon after the San Juan's junction with the Colorado, they tied up on a small beach where willows grew at the edge of immense cliffs.

"Let's go up and reconnoiter," the major suggested to his brother. Their problem was to find a suitable exit from the canyon. They saw a place that looked promising and swam the river to reach it, only to find that it led to a huge amphitheater in the rocks.

The ceiling of this vast enclosure contained a skylight. It had been carved out of the stone by a stream which they discovered when a sudden summer shower sent water through a hole in the cliff to form into a clear pool on its rocky floor.

In this lovely natural shelter, however, there were no solid clefts that could serve as footholds for climbing to the plateau above. Powell gave up further exploration for the moment and ordered the waiting members of his crew to cross over by boat and make camp in this great red-rock cave.

Entranced by the massive hall and the sweet sounds that wind and water produced within it, he named the place *Music Temple* and stayed over an extra day to savor it while he made observations and attempted another exit.

The climb was harrowing. There were only broken ledges on the cave walls which offered shaky holds at best, but he finally reached a point that afforded the view he needed to chart the area.

Glen Canyon displayed its full beauty to the river men during the next few days. They stopped often to walk up breathtaking side canyons. Several of these contained stands of oak and pine. Spring-fed streams gurgled down others. Some of the canyons provided stepping stones of water-washed rock that led up to a blue sky, contrasting vividly with the hues of the enclosing rock walls. There were many arches, and at one point a rainbow bridge of stone spanned a deep gulch, soaring high above the streambed. Forests of ferns and a brilliant array of wild flowers covered the floors of sheltered canyons.

On one of these side trips Powell fell upon an important piece of history that he had long sought to verify. During the journey he had kept a lookout for the spot where Father Escalante had crossed the river in 1776.

The Spanish priest had made his way north from Mexico to Santa Fe, the seat of government for Spanish New Mexico at that time. From there he had traveled northwest, crossing the Grand River in Colorado territory and the Green River from which the Powell party had started. On the return trip he had crossed the Colorado at a point where a stream came down from a side canyon to the west, spreading out as it reached a miniature valley.

When Powell's party entered this valley, they found proof of recent visits by Indians. Campfire ashes dotted the area. Scattered bones told of cattle, probably stolen from passing Mormon settlers, having been slaughtered and cooked by hungry tribesmen. A well-worn Indian trail led across the valley to a spot that was obviously used for fording the river. Noting these signs, the major decided that the priest and his party had found the crossing relatively easy during a time of low water. "This is it, *El Vado de los Padres,* the Crossing of the Fathers," he told his companions.

Soon after that historic find, the one hundred and forty-nine miles of Glen Canyon ended.

The explorers would never forget the colors of the cliffs — the vermilions, the rusts, the muted blues, the purples and pinks and creams, the orange and green spots, the rich chocolates and paler browns. An artist, using his choice paints, could not have prepared a richer palette. The canyon had renewed their spirits. It was to become their lasting memorial.

8

Point of No Return

MAJOR POWELL'S KNOWLEDGE of geology enabled him to "read" the rocks and gain some idea of what he might expect from the river. When softer rock formations appeared, his oarsmen found the water relatively calm. When it flowed between hard sandstone and limestone they encountered the same sort of dangerous rapids they had found in Desolation Canyon. His readings told him that the canyon they now approached would be a bad one.

They had scarcely entered it before they were caught up and carried downstream through a swirling rocky rapid. The canyon walls were straight up and down. They appeared impossible to scale, even if the boats could fight their way to shore, and they increased in height as the party was tossed along. "Falls ahead!" Powell signalled. "We'll have to portage."

With great effort the crews brought the boats up against a cliff face broken by a crevice over-head. Since it couldn't be reached from the deck of the *Emma Dean* directly beneath it, one of the men volunteered to stand on another's shoulders and pull himself up onto the little shelf of rock. This accomplished, a line was thrown to him and the major and two other men climbed the wall to join him. They hoped to gain a point above the falls where they could view the prospects for a portage, but they found the shelf suddenly broken off and the distance too great for them to leap safely.

"We'll have to bridge it," said Powell. "I saw some logs lodged in the rocks across the stream. You fellows take a boat and get them."

This, too, was a dangerous maneuver, but the

men took pride in besting the wild river. They handed the logs up and Major Powell walked across on them. He had to work his way higher and higher before he could get a satisfactory view of the falls below.

After careful planning they were able to transfer the boats. Their only advantage at this stage of the journey lay in their lack of provisions. Fewer packs had to be carried across the treacherous ledges.

An eclipse of the sun was to take place the next day and Powell was determined to make observations during this phenomenon. He had spotted a place where he thought he could climb to the top of the cliffs and he and his brother set out with his instruments slung over their backs. After four hours of very hard climbing they reached the summit, but by then clouds had blown in, obscuring the sky, and a rainstorm had developed.

Having regretfully missed the eclipse, they started back to camp. However, they found the descent much harder than the climb had been. The rocks had turned slippery in the rain and night fell early, multiplying the dangers. Stumbling down in zero visibility, they lost their bearings.

"We can't feel our way in the dark with this rain pouring down on us," Major Powell said. "We'll have to wait out the storm." That night seemed endless as they perched insecurely on a too-narrow ledge, but once the sun rose in a clear sky they hurried back to camp and a late breakfast.

Among his rock specimens the major placed several fragments of polished marble. "How many men have ever seen such beauty?" he asked. "Twenty-five hundred foot walls of solid marble! . . . Naturally, the name of this canyon shall be listed as *Marble*."

Their destination was to the west, but at one point in Marble Canyon the river turned sharply and ran eastward. The walls gleamed as though festooned with diamonds. On closer observation they found that the "diamonds" were sparkles made by the water coursing from the high rocks and spilling down the walls. They were to see this effect many times, for the summer rains had brought cascades of water from the plateau country above to plunge over the edge of the cliffs on their way to the river.

From maps made during his land expedition, Powell calculated that they should soon reach the mouth of the Little Colorado which he called the *Colorado Chiquito*. This was the furthest point he had charted. He was not sure what lay beyond.

They arrived on August 10 and stayed for two days while he measured latitude and longitude and estimated the height of the walls bordering this tributary to the Colorado. The men were busy drying out their provisions again, putting what remained of the flour through mosquito netting and boiling the bacon which was about to spoil beyond edibility.

When these chores were finished, they left camp to explore on their own. They found the same sort of cliff ruins and pottery that they had come across earlier in the month, as well as many more unreadable petroglyphs chipped into the cliff faces. It seemed evident that all along the river ancient Indian tribes had lived over long periods of time. Their history, however, was hidden in the past.

"These walls are three thousand feet high in spots," the major reported after finishing his calculations. "More than half a mile! And in some places they are absolutely vertical. Not even a mountain goat could find a foothold. . . . By the way, there are rattlesnakes in the area. I've killed two."

"We killed one at camp," the cook reported. "We'd best look where we walk here."

"Now we enter the 'Great Unknown,'" Powell told his men on the morning of August 13 as they prepared to board their boats. "We don't know how far it is to our destination. We don't know what falls and rapids we'll have to conquer. This is the moment we've been waiting for . . . Take off!"

He tried to sound confident, but he had deep misgivings. No one had ever emerged from the vastness of the uncharted Grand Canyon to tell his tale. If all went well, maybe. . . . It was self-defeating to think these thoughts, but he could not relish the rather grisly jokes the men made as they cast off. He was keenly aware of his responsibility for their lives.

His fears were realized within the next few miles. The area contained a great deal of lava, telling of volcanic activity in the past. The black snags rose like sharp teeth reaching up to destroy the men who had been so daring as to venture into their long-unvisited domain. The water was now running swiftly through the narrow gap of the canyon. They raced downstream, each moment filled with peril. The bottoms of their boats could be ripped out or the frail hulls crushed and they would be thrown into the maddened waves.

They came to a falls that thundered over some seventy-five feet of granite ledges. No portage was possible for the walls could not be scaled. Two choices remained. They must either ride it down or give up the project. Major Powell had no intention of turning back, and the men were willing to take their chances on the falls with him.

The waves played ball with them, tossing the boats back and forth until the *Emma Dean* was caught in a whirlpool and spun round like a top. Eventually it was thrown free but the open compartment was full of water and the boat was out of control.

The other boats made it safely to the bottom of the falls, and when the watching oarsmen saw that the *Emma Dean* was in danger, they pulled their boats into an eddy. As the swamped craft drifted past, they guided it to a bank to be bailed out. Their teamwork, each man working for the good of the others, had triumphed again.

"Look at those cliffs," Major Powell said after

they had reorganized. "They're a good mile high. Incredible!" The men looked and shuddered, imagining what it would be like to be trapped in the gloomy depths of the thrashing canyon that seemed to be trying every moment to rid itself of the foreigners.

The scenery was spectacular, but Powell had little time to enjoy it and he longed for a more leisurely view of the towers and buttes and pinnacles. As it was, he had to concentrate on making fast decisions.

Rapids and falls faced them with greater frequency, each one presenting its own problems. Sometimes the portages were simple matters, but more often they were so complex that it was a toss-up as to which plan would be the most successful.

The weather added to their troubles. It ranged from heavy rainfall to boiling sunlight to chilly darkness. One stormy night they were forced to make camp on a narrow ledge of rock. Food could not be hauled up from the boats and their tiny fire did not last long in the downpour. While lightning forked through the sky and thunder reverberated against the canyon walls, Powell and his men crouched on their ledge, hat brims pulled down and ponchos held tight to shut out some of the deluge.

In spite of all their efforts to navigate the river without accident, they came into another section of wild white water where the boats went out of control as great waves washed over them. One boat capsized and the occupants clung to its sides until they were rescued. Their oars were lost and a pair had to taken from the *Emma Dean* to put them back in action.

The next day nature granted the group a rest. They came to a clear stream that tumbled down a side canyon from the Kaibab Plateau to join the muddy, silt-laden Colorado, engorged just then with the run-off of recent rainstorms.

The stream provided fresh drinking water, and they made camp on a comfortable beach beneath an old shade tree. It did not seem so tragic in this soothing atmosphere that they had to throw away their bacon. Now they had only a little musty flour, some dried apples, and coffee to sustain them until the end of their journey. How many days this would take they did not know, but it seemed certain that it would be much longer than they had counted on at the beginning.

While the men worked a pine log into oars, Major Powell hiked up the stream to its head about six thousand feet above the river. On the way he found more crumbling houses, pottery, and other artifacts, including a great lava stone on which the Indians had ground their corn. Standing inside the walls of one of these ruins, he wondered again why these people had hidden themselves away in such remote places. Was it to escape the white men who were drifting up from Mexico, intent on conquering the mesa villages and converting the tribes to their own religion? Or were there other reasons that he might never learn?

"What shall we call this little river?" one of the men inquired when Powell returned from his hike.

"Well, Dunn," the Major smiled, "you named the Dirty Devil back there a way. How about us balancing things by calling this the *Bright Angel*?" The men approved the name. The stream was a bright spot on the trip which they would long remember.

They needed bright spots. The rains occurred more often, and their ponchos had been lost in the last river mishap. What canvas they still possessed was rotten and wouldn't shed water. They no longer had a blanket apiece and most of them had lost their hats along the way. The lack of substantial food was beginning to tell on their nerves and their strength. Accidents were so frequent that they were almost the order of the day.

In his diary Major Powell noted that the night of August 19 was the first cheerful time they had enjoyed for two weeks. They found a good supply of driftwood, made a roaring fire, and dried out their clothing and remaining supplies. This night was special because they could see stars instead of rain clouds.

The spirits of the party continued to rise as the weather turned clear, and they could once more observe the natural wonders they were passing. There was the beauty of Havasu Creek tumbling down the canyon in a veil of sparkling water with delicate ferns growing in a cave behind its falls. They came upon an extinct volcano which explained the many cinder cones and the hundred-foot pinnacles of lava they had seen. Huge springs poured from the rocks on the opposite side of the river from the volcano, and a dozen other scenes of geologic change delighted Powell and enriched his studies of earth's development.

On the morning of August 26 another sight stirred the entire crew to a high pitch of excitment — an Indian garden. The corn was not mature enough to be eaten as roasting ears, but squash was ripe on the vines growing among the corn stalks, and that squash looked irresistible to the starving travelers.

There were no signs of Indian guards, so they ran the boats over to the shore near the garden, gathered a good supply of the vegetables and hurried to a campsite to cook them. For the next few miles, restored by their feast, they felt they had faced the worst the canyon could give. They were wrong.

9

The Crisis

"THIS IS THE WORST YET!" The men were too busy steering to say more, but Major Powell knew they were right in their assessment of the situation. The black walls of another granite canyon loomed before them. Granite had, so far, spelled trouble, and this time they were deep in the heart of the Grand Canyon, their food almost gone and their possessions lost in the river.

Powell signalled for a stop and scrambled up the canyon wall. To proceed without reconnaissance of the area would be suicidal, but after climbing almost a mile, he still could not see what lay ahead, so he returned to the river.

A tiny stream came down from his left, promising better climbing possibilities. The boats tied up at its mouth while the men had a frugal noonday meal on the rocks. Then the major attempted another ascent.

As he reached a high point he heard a thunderous crashing below. Forgetting caution for an instant he edged along a slender shelf, his one hand secure in a crack of the granite wall above him. This movement trapped him when he came to a place which offered no footing for the next step and no possibility of turning around. The walls glowered above him and the raging river waited for him four hundred feet below. Powell yelled for help!

His men had already seen his predicament and several hurried to the rescue carrying two oars. He did not dare release his single hand-hold long enough to grasp a rope, so one man pressed an oar to the major's chest pushing him against the cliff, while another bridged the gap in the shelf with the other oar, enabling him to grab to a new hand-hold and swing to safety.

The sight that lay ahead was discouraging to Powell. It was absolutely terrifying to the men who had followed him up the cliff face. A dam of boulders rose from the river and a roiling waterfall plunged over it and ran to rapids with still another fall beyond. They had come this far, they told each other, only to be killed here in the great depths of the canyon.

Seneca Howland, his brother Oramel, and William Dunn resolved that they would leave the party rather than attempt such an impossible navigation. It was an unhappy decision, and not one of the three wanted to tell Major Powell how they felt. At last O. G. Howland spoke up.

"I'd like a word with you, Major," he said after the coffee had been boiled and savored along with a handful of dried apples, a little the worse for a coating of river silt.

Powell rose at once and sauntered down the sandy beach to the water's edge, sensing that what Howland had to say was private. "All right, my friend, what's on your mind?"

"Major, my brother and I — and Bill Dunn —

we've looked things over and we don't believe the boats can make it through this stretch. We think you should abandon the whole project. . . . Oh, I know how you've had your heart set on getting through and we all hoped you could make it. But, Major, we're not going. We're leaving you if you won't listen to reason. We want to save our lives!"

This lack of confidence on the part of his men was like a slap in the face for Powell. For a moment he could not speak. Then he said quietly, "I see . . . I haven't plotted our course for a couple of days. I'll do it now and let you know where we are."

It was a clear night, the stars growing brighter as darkness settled in. With his sextant, the major made painstaking calculations. Howland had fallen asleep beside a boulder by the time he had finished. Powell awakened him.

"I figure we're about forty-five miles from the mouth of the Rio Virgen," he said, spreading his map on the sand and holding a light above it. "I think there are Mormon settlements there. Of course, river miles are longer than this 'as-the-crow-flies' estimate, but counting twice as many miles would give us only ninety. . . . Think, man! We've come a long way. We've had brushes with death and come through in one piece. Do you think it's sensible to quit now? I've thought it out carefully. I'm not reckless. I believe we can run the rapids and portage over the falls. . . . It won't be easy but nothing on this trip has been easy. Don't say anything more tonight. Sleep on it and we'll talk in the morning."

"I know how you feel," Howland said regretfully, "but I know how I feel too. I want to get out of this canyon while I can. I don't like the look of those black walls and white waters. I don't like it at all."

With a sigh Major Powell got to his feet and found a sheltered nook where he bedded down for the night. But he could not sleep. For a time he lay looking at the stars and listening to the

peaceful snores of the men and the roar of the river. Then he got up and began pacing back and forth on the strip of sand where they had camped.

Was he being foolhardy and stubborn? Should he take his men out of here while he still could? Did it matter so much whether he ran this river and conquered the canyon?

Clearly it was a time for faith — faith in God and in his own judgment. In that dark night, with the stars flashing in the clear desert sky, Powell asked for guidance and found the strength and peace of mind to follow the course he had mapped.

Describing that part of the Grand Canyon in his diary he wrote: "There are cliffs where the soaring eagle is lost to view 'ere he reaches the summit. . . . Wherever we look there is but a wilderness of rocks; deep gorges where the rivers are lost below the cliffs, and towers and pinnacles, and ten thousand strangely carved forms in every direction. . . ."

The next morning he argued long and hard with the Howlands and Dunn while the other men listened glumly. "Major, you're crazy to try to put the boats over those falls!" Dunn said, and by the silence of his partners, Powell knew they agreed.

Then Seneca Howland changed his mind. "I'll stick it through," he said, "if the others will." But his brother and Dunn were anxious to be on their way.

When it became evident that the men could not be persuaded to continue the trip, Major Powell wrote a hasty letter to his wife and asked them to mail it for him. Sumner gave them his watch and asked them to turn it over to his wife if he was not heard from again. O. G. Howland was instructed to deliver a duplicate set of the records of the expedition to the proper authorities in the event that Powell and his remaining men should meet the doom predicted for them. The three refused to take any of the slim supply of food, saying they were certain to find game during the long walk, but they accepted two rifles and a shotgun.

Their departure was an emotional strain on everyone. Tough men though they were, they could not say good-bye without moist eyes and tight throats. They had been a team. Together they had met all the dangers the journey had thrown against them, and so far they had won. Now there was a feeling that they would not see each other again.

Major Powell suffered a second personal loss. The *Emma Dean* had taken a terrible beating from the river and was unusable unless constantly repaired. With three less men to handle the boats, one of them had to be abandoned. The *Emma Dean* was the logical choice, and so it was pulled up on the sand and its contents were transferred to the *Maid of the Canyon*. To lighten the loads for the passages ahead, Powell also left his precious barometer, his fossil collection, the mineral samples he had gathered, and some of the ammunition.

From a point far above, the Howlands and William Dunn watched the preparations. They shouted a farewell and were left behind as the two boats shot forward.

The rest of that day was a nightmare of effort. The water ran so swiftly, and the hidden rocks proved so treacherous that the boats were often wrenched from control of the steersmen. As the deserters had predicted, the party was faced with impossible hurdles time after time. Somehow, often by sheer accident, they forged ahead.

At one point Bradley, alone in the *Kitty Clyde's Sister,* shot a falls they had vainly attempted to portage earlier and disappeared into the fury of water below. Watching from surrounding crags, Powell and the others thought he was lost forever, but after what seemed an eternity, he and the boat surfaced to spin helplessly in a whirlpool.

The major sent Jack Sumner and Walter Powell down along the river's edge with lines to throw to Bradley. Then he boarded the *Maid of the Canyon* with Hall and Hawkins to follow Bradley's route over the falls. The boat tossed up and down in a frenzy of motion. It soon capsized, and Powell said later that all he knew about the short journey was that Bradley rescued them.

So it went all through that hectic day. Late in the evening, battered and exhausted, they came out of the granite cliffs. The toughest battle had been won!

10

Back to Civilization

AT NOON THE NEXT DAY they emerged from the Grand Canyon of the Colorado. They were the first white men — and probably the first men of any race — to complete the hazardous journey.

Their relief was so great that it reminded Major Powell of the agony he had suffered after losing his arm and the thrill he had felt when he was able to leave the hospital and smell the clean open fields once more. He rejoiced in the full expanse of sky instead of a narrow strip framed by dark canyon walls. The bird songs intensified, and the open land of the valley, which now bordered the river, offered a wonderful release from the sight of sheer stone.

It seemed very still now that the roar of the river had diminished. As they sat together that night in camp, they talked of their journey and of the three men who had left them. Where were they? Had they made it to a settlement? Had they found water and game, or were they starving and crazed with thirst?

"We'll begin searching for them the minute we meet someone who'll help us," Powell promised, knowing he could never rest until he had learned what had happened to them.

Meanwhile, the journey had to be completed. The men were more eager than ever to push on to the mouth of the Rio Virgen River and its promise of civilization. Their supplies had run out and they were living on nothing but determination.

They had gone only a few miles downstream the next morning when they glimpsed Indians running from the river's edge to hide in the rocks. Major Powell hailed them in a friendly manner, but they could not be lured back within sight of the boats.

In turning a sharp bend further on, they suddenly arrived at an Indian camp. This time, as the major called, "We come as friends," in their own language, a man, a woman and two naked children timidly remained in camp, although the others fled.

Powell gave an order to pull up to shore, and an unusual visit was made to these nomads of the desert lands. The Indians were shocked into silence but they stared at the equipment in the boats and studied the clothing of the river men.

The Indian man wore a hat over matted black hair which hung down over his shoulders. The woman's only apparel was a string of beads. She appeared concerned for the little ones who clung to her legs, half hiding behind her.

Their fright subsided when Major Powell mentioned the name of Jacob Hamblin, a Mormon who lived in the area, and they overcame their shyness long enough to beg for food and tobacco, but otherwise the visit produced no helpful information, and after a short stay the travelers proceeded down river.

"Any minute now . . ." Major Powell shouted as

he stood on deck to scan the widening river, "we'll see the mouth of the Rio Virgen — the rest of the way should be easy."

"Look!" One of his men pointed. "There's an Indian swimming ahead." The oarsmen rowed with new vigor. Soon they saw several people engaged in pulling something from the river.

"They're white men!" someone yelled, and so they were, except the swimmer. They were pulling in a seine loaded with fish.

"Ho, there!" the eldest of the three white men called. "Might you be the Powell party? . . . I thought so. Hamblin, he told us to be on the lookout for you — or your boats. That was a few weeks back. We didn't look to see you alive though! Join us in a meal. We made a good haul."

This was the point they had sought. Up the Rio Virgen were Mormon settlements where they could buy fresh food, clothing, and bedding, all sorely needed. From there they could send word to their anxious relatives and friends. They relaxed. The only note of unhappiness lay in their fears for the men who had quit them on the very brink of success.

"Have you any word of three men who left

our party two days ago? With any luck they should have shown up by now," the major asked while freshly caught fish broiled over an open fire.

The fishermen solemnly shook their heads. "Could be they ran into some hostile Indians," Asa, the spokesman, mused, and his sons nodded in agreement. "Some of these redskins are right friendly, like this boy we have with us today, but others. . . . We'll make some inquiries when we get back home in case word has got around. They'd try to get in touch with you, wouldn't they?"

"Yes," Powell said, his expression betraying his anxiety. "But if they survived, they'll be surprised to learn that we did, too. They didn't believe we could make it through the Grand Canyon. That's why they left us."

"Can't say I blame them," Asa replied. "Don't think anyone else thought you'd come out alive, except maybe Jacob Hamblin. He's a man that ain't afraid to tackle a brace o' wildcats if they try to stand between him and where he sets out to go."

"I've met him," Powell smiled. "I admire that man very much. Where is he?"

"Oh, he's around," Asa said vaguely. "Bishop Leithhead's in St. Thomas, about twenty miles up-

river. You might talk to him, but while you're here, you're welcome to what we've got at our place."

They sent the young Indian to St. Thomas with instructions to bring back whatever mail awaited them at its post office. When he returned he carried news that the bishop and other Mormons would arrive the next day with a wagon and supplies.

After three months on the river — three months of daily struggle with the wind and water, the storms and the summer heat — the sight of that wagon and the welcoming shouts of its riders seemed almost too good to be true. Along with other amenities of civilization, the wagon carried dozens of melons freshly picked from the gardens of Mormon frontiersmen.

Sumner, Bradley, Hawkins, and Hall decided to go on down to Fort Mohave by boat. "Then maybe we'll visit Los Angeles," one of the men laughed. "It won't be far and we've not seen much of city life lately."

Their high spirits made the moment of farewell less difficult for the major and his brother, Captain Walter Powell, who were going up to St. Thomas with Bishop Leithhead. From this small settlement they planned to travel to Salt Lake City where regular trains now ran to the East. They helped load the boats with sufficient supplies for the short ride and waved the four men on their way.

"It was a good trip, Major," Sumner said as he shook hands before the take-off. "I don't mind saying there were times when I somewhat questioned your decisions, but, by and large, they showed good sense and faith in what we could do if we tried. . . . I'd go along with you again, any day. Just you say the word."

This praise should have been comforting to Powell, but he turned away from the river with a troubled mind. The unknown fate of the Howlands and William Dunn weighed heavily upon him. Too many of his carefully compiled records had been lost. His scientific instruments had been damaged or abandoned. As he rode northward in the bishop's wagon, he began planning his next expedition.

11

The Fate of Three

IT WAS LATE AUGUST of 1869 when the first river passage of the Grand Canyon was completed. John Wesley Powell spent most of the next year organizing another expedition along the same route. His experiences during the first trip had convinced him that careful planning could eliminate many dangers. As part of this planning he decided to make another preliminary land survey of the country bordering the Colorado, especially the part he had not mapped during his 1867 overland trek.

"What we want to look for," he told some Mormon friends who had agreed to accompany him on the survey, "are spots where supplies can be brought to the river. If we can establish depots at intervals of 100 to 300 miles, we won't have to face near starvation along our way." He had spent a little over three months on the river the previous year, but he expected to extend his second voyage.

In early September of 1870, he began his land exploration at the headwaters of the Sevier River on a great plateau in the southwest corner of Utah. He hoped to find trails to the Colorado, leading down from the highlands of the north through steep side canyons.

The Sevier flows north into Sevier Lake, but on the southern slope of the plateau, the Rio Virgen, or Virgin, as it is called, flows south to the Colorado. It was at the mouth of the Virgin River that his river party had met the kindly fishermen. Now he planned to strike east to the Kanab waterway and on to the Paria, where he knew the river could be crossed.

Jacob Hamblin, the Mormon missionary who was so highly regarded by the Indians of that area, had persuaded several men of the Kaivavits tribe to make the trip with Powell. He hoped they could find trails unknown to the white man. Their chief, Chuarruumpeak, expressed doubts about reaching the river's edge but said his men could find waterholes for the explorers.

Magnificent pink cliffs rose before them when they started out, but it was a struggle for the men and horses to reach the top of the plateau. At one point the major walked blindly through mist and fog to the very brink of a precipice. The animals mired in the marshy ground and had to be pulled out with ropes. As the party forged through a tangle of wild rosebushes to wade a stream, they sank into quicksand up to their armpits. At every turn ledges, broken rock faces, and tumbled boulders slowed their pace.

The hardships of the trek did not dull Powell's appreciation for the beauty and importance of the landscape. His notebooks were filled with descriptions of the gold, purple, and red hills. He also made detailed entries concerning the geography of this great wilderness. He wanted the United States government to reap the benefits of this exploration while he satisfied his own great curiosity about the many-faceted Grand Canyon.

As he pushed forward he closely observed the Indians who had accompanied him. Each day he learned a few words of the guttural Kaivavits tongue and at night he tried out his growing vocabulary. It pleased the Indians to teach him their language and Powell had more than one reason for studying it.

When the time was right, he meant to ask their help in learning the fate of the Howlands and William Dunn. He had been warned that rushing them would close all doors. If they felt that he was trying to trap them or accuse them of wrong-doing, they might draw into themselves, or worse, leave the party completely.

Water, rocks, and dark canyons — these made up their daily fare. In places they traveled along streams where rock overhangs completely shut out the sky, or cliffs rose straight up leaving them only a narrow glimpse of the heavens. In some areas the canyon was fairly wide, but rock walls inclined inward, almost meeting at the top and enclosing the raging waters in a deafening roar.

They emerged from the gloom of one such canyon into a small valley. A Mormon town lay before them and a freight train had just pulled in hauling boxes of grapes and melons. Fresh produce was a real luxury for the tired travelers whose basic meals consisted of beans and bacon and sourdough biscuits.

Without the Indians' knowledge of mountain trails, Powell's exploration would have been finished almost before it began. Water was of prime importance to the men, their horses, and the pack mules. The Indians knew where to look for springs and potholes. It would have been totally frustrating to travel along, wilting with thirst, and see the stream below — at the foot of inaccessible cliffs.

The old chief had told Powell about a band of

Indians who lived near a deep pocket of water in a gorge, hidden from the sun and never dry. The gorge was carved on the side of a volcanic mountain heaped with broken lava and cinder cones, which made it hard to travel, but the major did not let that deter him.

When they reached a valley where these Indians sometimes camped, the party halted while the old chief went on to tell the nomads that the white men came in peace. The Indians, however, had warily scurried to hiding places in the rocks before the chief could talk to them. Only a woman remained. Caught by surprise as she gathered seeds and stored them in a wicker basket carried over her back, she seemed willing to talk. She told the chief that her people were in a nearby valley and that one of the men would run ahead to relay the message that the visitors were friendly.

A great fire was burning when the Powell party arrived at the encampment, and the strangers were greeted courteously by the curious villagers. After the evening meal more wood was piled on, and the Indians and explorers sat together around the cheerful blaze. "Fetch the tobacco," Powell told his Indian helper, and when it was brought from the packs, all the men took part in the ceremonial smoke. Talk would commence only after this period of quiet meditation.

Jacob Hamblin had earlier assured the Indians that this white man with only one arm did not come to take their land away but only to learn about the rivers and canyons, the mountains and plateaus. He had told them they could trust Major Powell, and since they trusted Hamblin they were not suspicious of the man who claimed him as a friend.

While the flames leaped higher they told Powell about their ways. Their women gathered sunflower seeds, grass seeds, and native plants bearing fanlike bunches of reeds. These they roasted and ground into a meal which was then cooked with a little water. They wove willow twigs together to form baskets for carrying the babies, and their clothing was made from the hides of animals they killed.

They had no guns, but they fashioned well-balanced flint and obsidian arrows. Stout bows were whittled to shoot these sharp projectile points. Rabbits were their main source of food, but sometimes they were fortunate enough to kill a deer or a mountain sheep and they made use of

every part of these animals — not only the meat
but the bones, sinews, hides, horns, and hoofs as
well.

One of the Indians told, with many gestures,
how they gathered grasshoppers on cold mornings
when the insects were too chilled to fly. The
women roasted them until they were bone-dry,
after which they were ground into meal and made
into a thick gruel which was considered a great
delicacy by the tribe.

Gradually, as they became used to having the
white men in their village, they talked more freely.
The older men told long, involved stories about
their forefathers and the gods they worshiped.

Major Powell asked them to send a messenger
to the Shivwits Indians, who lived in the vicinity.
He waited restlessly for an acceptance of his invi-
tation to join him for a friendly pow-wow.

When they arrived — a group of sharp-eyed,
athletic men carrying bows and arrows and dressed
in ragged buckskins — he greeted them formally
and invited them to sit down around the council
fire and smoke the pipe, a sign of peaceful inten-
tions.

"You can't rush these people," Hamblin's words

came back to him. "They'll talk, but only when they're ready. Rush things and they'll up and leave."

The Shivwits lived in the area the Howlands and Bill Dunn would have travelled, and Powell felt they might know what had happened to them. He could not rest until he found out, but patience had to be practiced for the moment.

He allowed the chief of the village to tell the Shivwits in their own language why his pale-faced guest was among them.

"*Kapurats,*" the chief used the Indian word meaning *man with one arm,* "came through the great waters of the river and through the darkness of the thundering canyon in a boat. He had other men with him. Three of them were afraid to ride with him. They climbed out of the canyon and have not been seen for twelve moons. Our friend, Jacob, says Kapurats is a man with a good heart. He does not want our lands. He will not come here digging for gold and silver. He wants to learn our way of talking and be our friend. He wants to help us get more to eat and wear. He wants to show us how to live warmer in winter and cooler in summer. He wants to know about trails — trails down

to the big river. These things are close to his heart."

The Shivwits listened in silence. For a long time they sat lost in their own thoughts. Then their chief spoke with them in quiet tones. After a prolonged interchange he addressed himself to Powell.

"Your talk is good," he nodded. "We believe you speak truth. We believe in Jacob. He is our father. You, too, will be our father. You may come into our land and eat our sweet fruit and our deer and rabbits. You may drink from our springs. We will tell the people on the other side of the great river that Kapurats is a friend of Jacob's and a friend of the Indians."

"Ask them about the men from my party," Powell begged his host. He could hold back this question no longer. The Indians were silent again, considering their reply. Then they spoke frankly.

"We killed three white men. We thought they were enemies. They came into our land. They were dying of thirst. We gave them water and fed them and they went away. Then bad men told us the palefaces had killed one of our women. We thought the bad men spoke truth. We were very angry. We followed the strangers and shot arrows into them. We took their guns and clothing . . . We have spoken. Now let us be friends."

Powell's heart ached for his murdered men but he understood the events that had led to their deaths. He could feel no real bitterness toward these primitive Indians. It was reasonable that they should have believed the lies of evil-doers since they could not accept the explanation of the men that they had come down the river in boats. This had never happened before in their lifetimes or in the lifetimes of their fathers. Now they knew they had killed innocent men, but it was too late to undo their vengeful deed. They had been honest about their actions.

"Let us be friends," Major Powell echoed these words in the Ute language, and again there was a solemn silence. He was certain they understood how he felt as he left the council circle.

In the gathering darkness he found a path fitfully lighted by the dancing campfire. He climbed to a cliff ledge a short distance away. Here he could be alone to mourn his dead companions.

12
Indian Country

IT HAD BEEN POWELL's plan to travel along the Colorado to the Paria River and cross there, if possible. Then he hoped to spend some time exploring Indian ruins and present-day villages on the south side of the Colorado.

On the way he climbed to one jutting rock from which he could see into the great depth of the Grand Canyon. The view so impressed him in its majestic proportions that, some years later, he took his artist friend, Thomas Moran, to the same spot. The picture Moran painted is today considered the most remarkable of the many Grand Canyon paintings.

Jacob Hamblin and two other white men had come with Powell to help in the river crossing. They made a raft on which the supplies and equipment were ferried across the muddy stream, sluggish during this early autumn. Powell and Hamblin, with Indian helpers, pushed on for Hopi territory — called *Tusayan* by the Spanish explorers — and arrived safely at the ancient village of Oraibi, which is said to date back to 1120 A.D.

They were pleased with their reception. The Hopi people then, as now, were peaceful farming Indians. They lived, like their ancesters, in terraced rock houses built on the crests of rocky mesas.

Powell was impressed by the Hopis' culture. After the wild, unclothed Unikarits, and other tribes on the north side of the canyon, these people were remarkably civilized.

They called the headman of the village who came at once and set aside several rooms for the use of the visitors. They entered by climbing a

ladder to the first terrace, then descending another
ladder into their rooms. The weather was warm
and there was no need for fires, but fireplaces had
been built into one corner of each room and little
stacks of juniper were brought for them, should
they care for more heat.

They stayed several days in the village while
Powell made notes on the habits and dress of the
people, their diets and methods of food prepara-
tion. For the first time he tasted *Piki,* a paper thin
cornbread made by the women from a paste of
hand-ground meal, swished over a hot piki stone
to cook it. The harvest had been good that year.
There were melons — a food much loved by the
Hopi — peaches off their little trees grown from
peach pits the Spanish conquistadores had brought
to the Indian country, and an ample supply of
goat and mutton stew.

From Oraibi they went on to visit the other
Hopi villages of Shungopavi, Michongnovi, Shupaulovi, Walpi, Sichumovi, and Hano.

Powell would long remember the call of the
town crier that first morning in Oraibi. He was
summoning the people to prayers at the mesa
edge. They came, men, women, and children,

carrying cornmeal over which they breathed their prayers for a good life and rain for their gardens. They then flung the sacrifice of meal toward the rising sun.

He also witnessed their ritual of morning cleansing. After they had washed their hands and faces, they cleaned their long black hair and dressed it in the fashion of the tribe.

With open hearts they shared their best with the explorers, and through interpreters they told Powell many stories of their ancestral ways. They had already learned of his successful boat trip through the fearful canyon and looked up to him as a man of great courage to be admired and honored.

At Shupaulovi, Powell and his friends were invited to witness a ceremonial dance, performed, like most Hopi dances, as a prayer for rain. Their homes were in an arid country and their gardens often bordered the edges of sand dunes. Rain was their salvation. Without it they would have to endure long periods of near-starvation.

Powell had brought many articles which would be useful to the Hopis. He intended to exchange his bright cloth, scissors, awls, needles and thread, knives, and paints for their handcraft.

The Indians' eyes glittered at the array he laid before them. They loved to barter and were skilled at the art of trading. Powell was able to secure many fine specimens of pottery, masks, baskets, shoulder blankets, rabbit-skin quilts, and shell and turquoise ornaments.

Michongnovi and Shupaulovi occupy one mesa, Oraibi another, and Walpi, Schumovi, and Hano a third. Of all the Hopi villages, Walpi presents the greatest problems of approach. Present-day mesa dwellers can use their cars and pickup trucks on the good road that has been built up its steep slope, but in Powell's time there was only a trail with the steepest pitches made into a series of steps.

Walpi itself rises in uneven steps of rock from a sheer stone platform at the end of a narrow promontory thrusting out into the desert. The village is concentrated at that point and is approached across a very rocky "neck" that joins it to the body of the mesa where its sister rock cities have been built.

Walpi and Sichumovi are very old towns, dating back to times prior to the arrival of the Spanish in Tusayan, but Hano is comparatively new and peopled by men and women of the Tewa tribe of New Mexico, who speak a language unlike that of the Hopis among whom they now live.

While he was in Walpi, Powell was told about the snake dance held each summer. The most spectacular of all the Hopi ceremonial dances, it, too, is a prayer for rain.

Major Powell's long visit on the Hopi mesa proved rewarding from many standpoints. He had gathered a fine collection of articles representing their culture. The October weather was beautiful and clear, producing the deep golden sunsets for which that area is noted. He had managed to learn a few key words of the difficult Hopi language and had discovered a great deal about the living conditions of the southwest Indians. He was determined to make his knowledge public. Too many white men had pushed the Indians aside, reluctant even to acknowledge their presence, let alone consider their rights.

The plight of these people was most forcefully impressed upon Powell when he left Pueblo territory and came into the red-canyon country of the Navajos. His guide on this trek was a fine looking

Navajo with black eyes and a beaked nose. He wore necklaces of rough turquoise, mother-of-pearl, and colored beads, a "concho" belt of silver strung together with leather thongs, and a bright shirt and leggings of black velvet. His moccasins were adorned with silver, and silver ornaments trimmed his horse's bridle.

Their destination was Fort Defiance, the agency of the Navajo reservations. Powell wanted to help Jacob Hamblin persuade the Navajo people to make a friendship treaty with the Mormon settlers.

At Fort Defiance thousands of the tribesmen had gathered to receive rations from the government. There was a festive air to the horse racing, dancing and singing that went on, but the Navajos' hatred of the white men was reflected in their faces. They had only recently been allowed to return to their beloved mountains and canyons after a four-year period of imprisonment at Bosque Redondo in New Mexico. The suffering and anguish they had endured on the "Long Walk" they had been forced to make was still a raw wound in their minds.

Powell and Hamblin sought out Barboncito, a

tall, eloquent headman of the Navajos. They talked with him and some of his council leaders at great length, and this meeting produced an agreement that the Navajo tribe would be friends to the Mormons.

Continuing his travels through Indian country, Major Powell visited the Zuñi pueblos in New Mexico and found them much like those of the Hopis. Here, as usual, he spent much of his time studying the language of the Zuñi people. It was a distinctly separate tongue, not at all like the language of the Hopis or the Navajos.

Early in November, his survey of the great valley of the Colorado River completed to his satisfaction, the major headed northward. His mind was now occupied with planning for a second river expedition through the Grand Canyon.

13

The Second Expedition

To HIS SURPRISE Powell found that he had become a national hero. Newspapers and magazines clamored for more and more details about his fabulous conquest of the Grand Canyon. When he requested government backing for a second expedition, it was quickly approved. The president and other federal officials were eager to support his new project.

Major Powell had been disappointed, to a great degree, with the first expedition. He had seen his carefully prepared scientific calculations disappear into the waters of the Colorado. He had lost three valuable men because of their lack of faith in his judgment. This wounded him far more deeply than others suspected.

On the positive side, he had gained much more than the momentary fame given him by an admiring people. He had learned to know and sincerely care for the Indians of the wilderness areas, and he had resolved to learn more before their ancient cultures were swept away by the tides of a new civilization. Very few people considered them important enough to merit study.

As he planned for his second expedition, Powell's thoughts were often concerned with the education and welfare of Indians. How could he best present their grievances to a hostile world that seemed determined to ignore them and their problems?

He had traveled through Indian country without a gun and without fear. No one had attempted to harm him. With very few exceptions, the Indians had welcomed him as a friend and generously shared their food and belongings, pitifully small though they were.

To repay them in part for their kindnesses,

Powell wanted to classify the various tribes, their languages, and rituals. This might provide a basis for better understanding of their cultures.

First and foremost, John Wesley Powell was a man with a fertile mind. One idea was certain to develop into others, related and unrelated, but each one worthy of examination. He was much too busy working out his schemes to become vain or selfish, and he encouraged his friends to share his visionary dreams. He knew it would take more years than he would live to bring many of these dreams to reality.

"Knowledge," he once said, "is for the welfare of all the people." He gave freely of his own considerable knowledge, hoping others would pass it on for the good of future generations.

The members of the new expeditionary party gathered on the morning of April 29, 1871, at Green River City, Wyoming, where the first group had embarked in 1869. Powell's lead boat was again named the *Emma Dean.* The second boat was named *Nellie Powell,* in honor of Mrs. Nellie Powell Thompson, the major's sister and wife of Professor Almon Harris Thompson, who was to be Powell's assistant in charge of mapping the terrain they would travel. The third boat was appropriately called *Cañonita*. Major Powell was the only member of the first expedition to make the second trip.

Other members of the party included Frederick Dellenbaugh, a relative of the professor; Stephen V. Jones, John F. Steward, Captain Francis M. Bishop, Andrew Hattan, John K. Hillers, Frank Richardson, Walter Clements Powell, a cousin of the major; and E. O. Beaman, a photographer. Mrs. Powell and Mrs. Thompson went on to Salt Lake City to wait for their husbands to emerge from the canyon.

Dellenbaugh, seventeen years old and a self-taught artist, was to become the first painter of the Grand Canyon's wonders, and Beaman was the first photographer to capture the high cliffs and raging river on film. Dellenbaugh, some thirty-seven years later, published a pictorial account which illustrated not only the dangers and trials of the journey, but many of the relaxed and amusing moments the party enjoyed.

Although the men arrived at the take-off site in April, it was May 22 before work on the boats was completed and all the supplies and instruments safely packed. Powell's experiences on the initial journey had proved to him that only by the greatest efforts of organization could the records and other vital articles be saved from the onslaught of the river.

An arm chair was added to the middle deck of the *Emma Dean* so the major could ride comfortably while he conned the river for danger spots and alerted the oarsmen in back of him. Preventing damage to the boats was crucial. Each boat carried a third of the food which must serve the men for the greater part of the long ride.

This was to be a thoroughly scientific venture and the men made use of every valuable moment for observation. Along the way the professor and his assistants mapped the rivers, canyons and plateaus, while Powell researched the geologic features of the area.

They traveled by boat only as far as Lee's Ferry at the mouth of the Paria River. That fall they set up headquarters at the little Mormon town of Kanab, Utah, and explored the topography of the country from that base. They did not return to the Colorado River until August 1, 1872, almost a year later. Then for over a month they experienced the thrills and terrors of canyon cataracts, falls and rapids and came out of the canyon at Kanab Creek on September 7.

Powell had decided that it was too dangerous and no longer necessary to attempt the last stretch of the canyon. Instead, they spent the next three months exploring the Shivwits Indians' homeland on a vast plateau and returned to Kanab for final work on the great master map of the country. Frederick Dellenbaugh made a heroic journey through a February snowstorm to take the map to Salt Lake City where it could be sent on to Washington, D. C. The previous November, Powell had brought his wife, their baby, Mary, born in September, her nursemaid, and Mrs. Thompson to the Kanab camp where they remained until the work was finished.

A monumental task had been completed and Professor Almon Thompson had made a tremendous contribution in his tedious, dangerous, and exhausting work of solving, as Dellenbaugh said later, "the last geographical problem of the United States."

It was the sharp vision of John Wesley Powell, however, that gave life to the entire project. His first small expedition into the wilderness had spurred him to make this second journey, which produced the first accurate charts of an almost unknown territory.

14

Benefactor of His Country

As POWELL PREPARED for his return to the East, circumstances led him to an even deeper involvment in the Indian situation. An unworthy Indian agent had mistreated the Paiutes so severely that they threatened to go on the warpath. A new agent was sent out, but when he arrived he found that his predecessor, in a final effort to undo his damage, had made promises to the Indians that could not possibly be fulfilled. The uprising seemed inevitable and the Mormon settlers were certain to suffer unless something could be done.

Jacob Hamblin, who had seen Powell sway the uneasy Navajos with his eloquence and sincerity, asked him to appear at a council at Kanab, Utah. Word was sent out, and the Paiutes came in great numbers to hear what *Kapurats*, One-Arm-Off, had to say. He promised he would talk to government officials and "spare no effort to help them."

Hurrying back to Washington, he launched a bitter attack on the Bureau of Indian Affairs for its inhumane treatment of government charges. He made public his personal observations at many Indian reservations in Colorado, New Mexico, Arizona, and Utah. His statements testified to the mercilessness with which the Indians had been forced by the military onto barren stretches of land without means of irrigation.

He stressed the hopelessness of the Indians' fate. "These people," he said, "are human beings. They suffer pain and hunger and losses as keenly as we do. They should not be doomed to starvation and death through governmental disinterest. Their ancient cultures should be preserved for our enlightenment now and in the future."

Many people approved his compassionate stand on the Indian problem, but some officials of the Indian Bureau were angered and immediately began a campaign to discredit his claims. Powell stood up to the worst of their attacks. He had visited the Indians, he told them. He spoke from personal knowledge. He had traveled with Indian guides and packers and found them hard-working and trustworthy. He had not carried a gun to keep them in order, but had walked among them in dignity and without fear.

He told of how, one night at his western camp, fires were seen flashing from surrounding mountain peaks, and the Indians of his party became very agitated. He later learned that the signal fires had told the tribesmen that a survey party, accompanied by soldiers, had entered Nevada and killed one Indian and blinded another. He suggested to the government that surveying and exploratory parties travel without military guard, since this inflamed the Indians who would otherwise allow the white men to pass through their lands without trouble.

After much controversy Powell was appointed head of a commission to make what was called *A*

Special Study of the Problems of the Paiutes and Other Tribes in Utah, Colorado and Nevada. Again he headed west to open new doors for the Indians.

On this trip Major Powell met the artist, Thomas Moran, and spoke so glowingly of the Grand Canyon's beauties that Moran joined Professor Thompson at his Kanab headquarters. The artist eventually made the huge oil painting called "Grand Canyon of the Colorado," still considered the best canvas on that subject.

Powell's long study of the conditions of the Indians convinced him that he must persuade Congress to set up a Bureau of Ethnology. He planted the seed, but it was six years before it took root. Then he was named director of the newly created bureau. He was well prepared for the task. During the interval he had continued his studies of Indian languages and had compiled vocabularies as he visited the many tribes. He gathered more information on Indian ceremonies, folklore and ancient working tools. These pursuits, however, did not exclude his continuing interest in geology and geography.

He had devoted much time and thought to the problems of the settlers who had listened to glow-

ing promises of land developers and had traveled
west with their families and meager belongings to
stake out homesteads. "Rain follows the plow" was
the popular slogan they had believed to their ulti-
mate distress. They plowed but rain did not follow. Now and then a farmer harvested a crop.
More often, the land and the seed blew away.

Powell went before a meeting of the Committee on Public Lands. Using his maps he showed
them that "about two-fifths of the entire area of
the United States has a climate so arid that agri-
culture cannot be undertaken without irrigation."
He pointed out that the larger rivers, like the Colorado, could be used to provide the necessary water.
This would be a monumental task and the dams
could only be constructed with the cooperation
and backing of the federal government.

Powell drew on his vast accumulation of facts
and figures to warn the committee that the West
was being stripped by the greedy. If lumbermen
were allowed to cut timber at will, the forests, and
thus the watersheds, would be ruined. If cattle-
men were allowed to obtain land for a few cents
an acre, there would be no room for settlers seeking homes and land they could farm.

He incorporated these findings into a book called *Arid Lands,* which was filled with data from his travels and his own deductions, based on the geology of the western area. This book caused a furor. He was accused of trying to halt settlement with half-baked schemes.

Those who were loudest in their condemnation called the West a "paradise." Powell must have sighed over their ignorance as he recalled the hardships of his many journeys through that rugged land of mountains and canyons and cliffs.

Eventually the opposition subsided and level-headed members of Congress, after careful consideration of his book, acted to right some of the wrongs that had already affected the West.

It was logical for Powell to be named assistant to the Director of the National Geological Survey when that vacancy came up. He served conscientiously in that post, at the same time continuing his work for the Bureau of Ethnology. In the spring of 1881, President Garfield named him Director of the National Geological Survey.

In setting up the Bureau of Ethnology, Powell had enlisted the help of many skilled men, who worked without salary. They were instilled with the same fervor that motivated Powell. As Director of the Geological Survey his enthusiasm again attracted dozens of scientists willing to assist him for no pay except the rewards that came from working on vital projects with a man of such superior intellect and wide interests.

All this time Powell was writing on the subjects he had studied so thoroughly. His works sold well but never made him any great amount of money. Wealth was a matter of indifference to him. His chief concern lay in trying to finish the many projects he had taken upon himself through the years.

Even after he became known as a ranking American scientist and was elected President of the American Association for the Advancement of Science, he continued to dress and live plainly. He had no self-pride or egotism in spite of his many accomplishments. His explorations and laboratory experiments were his life. In the laboratory of the Geological Survey he supervised experiments which proved to his satisfaction that the entire chemical industry would one day be based on the use of petroleum. Another series of experiments with metals was so important that it led to the establishment of the Bureau of Mines.

Major Powell had successfully battled the elements, but in his later years he was attacked by men intent on stripping him of his powerful influence. By the time he reached sixty, he was worn out from his years of ceaseless work. His arm gave him constant pain and he was told that only another operation would relieve him. On May 4, 1894, he handed in his resignation from the bureau and went into a hospital. He recovered from the surgery but developed serious heart trouble, and the last eight years of his life were spent very quietly.

As America entered the twentieth century, Congress finally took action on land and water resource proposals for the West. Dams were to be built with government planning and funding, just as Powell had urged in *Arid Lands*. A bill creating a Bureau of Reclamation went into effect in June of 1902. At about the same time President Theodore Roosevelt was affixing his signature to the measure, Major Powell suffered a massive heart attack.

When he died the following September, famous men from all walks of life gathered at his funeral service. He and his brother-in-law, Almon Thompson, his most valuable assistant, lie buried in Arlington National Cemetery with other great Americans.

More than a hundred years have passed since John Wesley Powell and his first river party conquered the Grand Canyon of the Colorado. History records Powell as one of America's greatest explorers, and his remarkable feats still captivate adventurous minds. Many monuments have been built in his honor, but one seems particularly fitting for it pays homage to his far-reaching visions of the potential natural resources of the West. Near Page, Arizona, a great dam contains the life-giving waters of Lake Powell, artificially created from the river that flows through beautiful Glen Canyon.

Bibliography

Acknowledgment:
Help received from the following historical records and other publications listed is gratefully acknowledged by the author:

CORLE, EDWIN
   The Story of the Grand Canyon, New York: Duell Sloan & Pearce, 1951

DARRAH, WILLIAM CULP
   Powell of the Colorado, Princeton: Princeton University Press, 1951

DELLENBAUGH, FREDERICK S.
   A Canyon Voyage, New Haven: Yale University Press, 1926

POWELL, JOHN WESLEY
   The Exploration of the Colorado River, Garden City, New York: Doubleday and Company, Inc. (Abchor Books), 1962

POWELL, JOHN WESLEY
   The Exploration of the Colorado River and its Canyons, New York: Dover Publishers, Inc., 1961

STEGNER, WALLACE
   Beyond the Hundredth Meridian and the Plateau Province, Boston: Houghton Mifflin Company, 1954

TERRELL, JOHN UPTON
   The Man Who Rediscovered America, New York: Weybright and Talley, 1969

WHARTON, DON
   Utah, Fantasy in Sand and Stone, Reader's Digest, November 1969

WIBBERLEY, LEONARD
   Wes Powell, Conqueror of the Colorado, New York: Farrar, Straus and Cudahy, 1958 (Ariel Books)

WIDDISON, JERROLD G.
   John Wesley Powell, Man of Vision, Phoenix, Ariz.: Arizona Highways, May 1969

About the Author

Vada Carlson's knowledge of the American West, of Indian cultures and of the pioneers who explored and settled the area make her an ideal author for the exiting biography of John Wesley Powell. Mrs. Carlson, who lives in Winslow, Arizona, has received many honors and awards for her writings, including the *Women of Achievement Award* from the National Federation of Press Women. Two other books by her have recently been published by Harvey House — *Cochise, Chief of the Chiricahuas* and *John Charles Frémont, Adventurer in the Wilderness*.

About the Artist

Richard Cuffari's creative talents are found in the illustrations of over eighty books for young people, and have been awarded honors from the Society of Illustrators, The American Institute of Graphic Arts, and The Christophers. Mr. Cuffari studied art at the Pratt Institute. He makes his home in Brooklyn, New York, with his wife and their four children.